POETRY CO

GREAT MINDS

Your World...Your Future...YOUR WORDS

From Co Down
Edited by Heather Killingray

First published in Great Britain in 2005 by:
Young Writers
Remus House
Coltsfoot Drive
Peterborough
PE2 9JX
Telephone: 01733 890066
Website: www.youngwriters.co.uk

All Rights Reserved

© Copyright Contributors 2005

SB ISBN 1 84602 080 8

Foreword

This year, the Young Writers' 'Great Minds' competition proudly presents a showcase of the best poetic talent selected from over 40,000 up-and-coming writers nationwide.

Young Writers was established in 1991 to promote the reading and writing of poetry within schools and to the youth of today. Our books nurture and inspire confidence in the ability of young writers and provide a snapshot of poems written in schools and at home by budding poets of the future.

The thought, effort, imagination and hard work put into each poem impressed us all and the task of selecting poems was a difficult but nevertheless enjoyable experience.

We hope you are as pleased as we are with the final selection and that you and your family continue to be entertained with *Great Minds From Co Down* for many years to come.

Contents

Abbey Grammar School

Robert Crawford (13)	1
Colm Thompson (11)	1
Niall McCartan (12)	2
Niall Daly (12)	2
Michael Courtney (12)	3
Turlough Tinnelly (13)	3
J B Farrell (12)	4
Mathew Guy (12)	5
Brendan Reid (13)	6
Cormac Clerkin Parr (13)	6
James Hasson (13)	7
Éoin Mulvaney (13)	7
Adam Kane (12)	8
Eoin Colgan (13)	8
Dermot Markey (12)	9
Matthew Small (11)	9
Patrick Quinn (13)	10
Paul McShane (12)	10
Ethan Toner (13)	11
Ryan Quigg (12)	11
Jack McShane (12)	12
Ciaran McEvoy (12)	12
Michael Beswick (13)	13
Colum Gildea (12)	13
Michael Vallely (13)	14
Christopher Quinn (12)	15
Daniel McCormick (12)	16
Sean McDonnell (12)	17
Tony Fearon (13)	18
Oliver Hearty (13)	18
Sean Fegan (12)	19
Ryan Devlin (12)	19
Aodhan Byrne (11)	20
Sean McMahon (13)	21
Owen Carragher (12)	22
Michael McKevitt (12)	23
Conor Murtagh (13)	24
Steven Fearon (12)	25

David Hudson (13)	25
Patrick Gallogly (12)	26
Sean McCaffery (12)	26
Ryan Hudson (13)	27
Owen Jones (11)	27
Stephen Doherty (11)	28
Oisin McGuinness (11)	28
Kevin Gribben (12)	29
Oisín Lynch (11)	29
Glenn McConville (12)	30
Patrick McConville (12)	31
Rory Devlin (11)	32
Rory Keenan (11)	32
Garbhan McKevitt (12)	33
Scott Gray (11)	33
Liam Gray (11)	34
Kevin Quinn (11)	34
Conor Carroll (11)	35
Conor McKinley (12)	35
Cian Gallagher (12)	36
James Morgan (12)	37
Martin Hearty (11)	38
Peter Hollowood (11)	38
Daniel McCullagh (11)	39
Fergal McEvoy (11)	39
Christopher Fearon (12)	40
Colum Mackey (12)	40
Patrick Burns (11)	41
Matthew McGivern (11)	41
Deaglan O'Neill (12)	42
James O'Gorman (11)	42
Gavin O'Hare (11)	43
David Morgan (12)	43
Ryan O'Hare (11)	44
Conor McVeigh (11)	44
Brian Comaskey (11)	45
Jason Gray (11)	45
Mark Rocks (12)	46
Stephen O'Hare (11)	46
Dermot McVeigh (12)	47
Jordan Havern (11)	47
John-Joe Aitken (11)	48

Rory Devlin (12)   48

Ardmore House Special School
Daniel Campbell (14)   49

Clifton Special School
Tina Mairs (18)   49
James Skelton (17)   50
Kathy Galway (17)   51
Dave Gordon (16)   52
Robyn Loyer (16)   52
David Morton (16)   53

Glastry High School
Holly Chambers (11)   53
Graeme Warden (12)   54
Junita Coffey (11)   54
Hazel Montgomery (12)   55
Kirsty Mills (12)   55
Rebecka McCormick (11)   56

Glenlola Collegiate School
Emma Kyle (13)   56
Sarah Blair (12)   57
Leah Kirkwood (13)   57
Melissa Keenan (14)   58
Katherine McKnight (11)   58
Jenny Gwynne (14)   59
Gemma Wingar (14)   60
Emma Webster (14)   60
Lauren Scott (14)   60
Natassia Young (14)   61
Holly Clark (14)   61
Becky Smyth (14)   61
Tara Baird (12)   62
Ashley Martin (14)   62
Laura-Jane Stacey (13)   63
Emily Allen (12)   63
Rachel Graham (17)   64
Sarah McVeigh (18)   64

Alison McKibben (18)	65
Tory Hughes (16)	65
Kathryn Hunter (13)	66
Sarah Macauley (14)	66
Rachel Atwell (13)	67
Abi Ballantine (13)	67
Anna Harmon (17)	68
Megan McCreedy (13)	68
Ashley Thompson (17)	69
Tanya Baker (16)	69
Karina Magee (11)	70
Claire MacDuff (17)	70
Sian Brennan (13)	71
Carmen Tang (14)	71
Rebecca Bingham (13)	72
Lauren Scott (14)	72
Elizabeth Patterson (17)	73
Rachael Prentice (14)	73
Alison Rea (14)	74
Gillian McBride (12)	74
Jayne McKee (15)	74
Abbi McCallum (12)	75
Rebekah Heath (13)	75
Julie Scott (14)	76
Claire Boardman (13)	76
Claire Stannage (14)	76
Rebekah Hammond (13)	77
Sarah Brennan (17)	77
Jannine Macfarlane (14)	78
Rachel Pritchard (14)	78
Cassie Murphie (15)	78
Loren McDowell (14)	79
Nicole Mailey (12)	79
Kerry Adrian (13)	79
Megan Gray (17)	80
Rebecca Lennie (12)	81
Rebecca Blair (12)	81
Anna Baird (12)	82
Hannah Beattie (13)	82
Carly MacBratney (13)	82
Holly Hunter (13)	83
Lucy Kayes (13)	83

Monique Geddis (14)	83
Deborah Kinghan (13)	84
Hannah Steenson (15)	84
Ruth Hooks (14)	85
Etta Stevenson (15)	85
Heather Penn (16)	85
Nicola Durieux (17)	86

Kilkeel High School

Juneve Clark (14)	86
Rebecca Cassidy (16)	87
Emma Jane McCavery (16)	87
Louise Orr (15)	88
Alison McConnell (16)	88
Linda Clements (15)	89
Hollie Donaldson (11)	89
Grace Hanna (16)	90
Gareth Allen (15)	90
Donna Thompson (16)	91
Louise Campbell (13)	92
Chloe McCullough (11)	92
David Hanna (11)	93
Christopher Cousins (11)	93
Stephanie McDowell (16)	94
James Irvine (11)	94
Daryl Parke (16)	95
Nadine Hewitt (16)	96
Joshua Haugh (11)	96
Kerri Nicholson (11)	97
Mark Cromie (14)	97
Sarah Jane Conn (14)	98
Chris Charleton (12)	98
Andrew Clements (17)	99
Diane McMurray (14)	100
Joanna Reilly (12)	100
Neil Newell (12)	101
Danielle Rogers (14)	101
Rachel Nicholls (15)	102
Ryan Cunningham (13)	102
Emma Campbell (16)	103
Lauren Shields (13)	103

Katherine Beck (13)	104
Roberta Graham (15)	104
John Graham (13)	105
Andrew Smyth (14)	105
Ruth White (13)	106
Kathryn Jess (11)	106
Daniel Ogle (14)	107
Alex Russell (12)	107
Laura Shannon (15)	108
Laura Herron (11)	108
David Glenny (13)	109
Laura Hanna (16)	109
Ryan McAtee (13)	110
Philip Main (13)	110
Leanne McConnell (14)	111
Laura Beck (15)	112
Claire Annett (14)	113
Ruth Shannon (14)	114
Andrew Greene (13)	114
Rebecca McKee (15)	115
Claire Quinn (15)	115
Emma Annett (17)	116
Philip Gordon (13)	116
Steven Moorehead (14)	117
Jordan McConnell (15)	117
Jan McMurray (13)	118
Gary Bingham (13)	118
Stephanie Annett (16)	119
Rodney Watterson (13)	119
April Bridges (13)	120
Jason Tremlett (13)	120
Amanda Wilson (13)	121
Gemma Coulter (14)	122
Rebekah Patterson (14)	123
Ben Firth (13)	124
William Robert Hutchinson (12)	124
Rachael Quinn (14)	125
Naomi Shannon (11)	125
Leanne Shields (14)	126
David Beck (11)	126
Ruth Shields (14)	127
Darren James Haugh (13)	127

Grace Maginnis (18)	128
Laura Smyth (12)	128
Catherine Orr (17)	129
Paul Maybin (15)	129
Alan Robinson (15)	130
Elizabeth Keown (12)	130
Kirsty Morris (14)	131
Terence Huddy (14)	131
Linsey Wilson (16)	132
Lynn Maybin (16)	132
David McIlroy (16)	133
William Nugent (17)	133
Claire Johnston (14)	134
Rachel Curran (11)	134
Kirsty Lewis (17)	135
Kirstie Graham (15)	135
Zoe Nicholson (16)	136
Karen Moore (15)	137
Kelly Whyte (17)	137
Laura Baird (15)	138
Matthew Monaghan (15)	138
Mary-Jane McBride (12)	139
Donna Morris (14)	139
Julianne Megaw (16)	140
Courtney McClean (11)	140
Laura Agnew (12)	141
Lisa Newell (11)	141
Andréa Hanna (15)	142
Jourdan Lyons (12)	142
Laura Wortley (17)	143
Katherine Boucher (15)	144
William McKee (15)	144
David Pue (11)	144
Andrew Johnston (12)	145
Peter Quinn (12)	145
Alice Gordon (12)	146
David Holmes (12)	146
Linda Cargin (15)	146
Rebecca McDowell (11)	147
Mark McCullough (11)	147
Gemma Teggarty (11)	148
Megan Holmes (11)	148

Melissa McConnell (11)	149
Harry Reilly (11)	149
David Henning (12)	149
Adam Nicholls (14)	150
Aimee Johnston (11)	150
Christine Haugh (13)	151
Gregor Strachan (12)	151
Laura Campbell (12)	152
Jake Pulford (12)	152
Amy Bingham (13)	153
Elizabeth Morris (12)	153
Robert Tomkins (11)	154
Andrew Wilson (11)	154
Richard McKee (15)	154
Alex Speers (13)	155
Nicola Bell (12)	155
Ashley Cracknell (13)	156
Emma Connor (12)	156
Michelle Skillen (12)	156
Kerri Elizabeth Graham (13)	157
Lesley Gordon (11)	157
Jane Annett (14)	158
Wendy Hanna (15)	158
Lauren Baird (12)	159
Julie Annett (13)	159
Jennifer McConnell (14)	160
Euan McCracken (12)	160
Emma Tremlett (13)	161
Kathy Newell (13)	161
Sandra Baird (14)	162
Lynette McCavery (13)	163
Nadine McConnell (13)	164
Jenny Cunningham (13)	164
Amy Dodds (13)	165
Adrian McCullough (13)	165
Diane Graham (15)	166
Jonathan McCulla (15)	166
Sarah Graham (15)	167
Leanne Newell (17)	168
Kirk Whyte	168
Rachael Bleakley (17)	169
Sara Holmes (15)	169

Kathryn McCullough (14)	170
Laura Annett (15)	170
Deborah Hanna (18)	171
Emma Teggarty (17)	172
Warren Nugent (13)	172
Mark Stevenson (15)	173
Mark Campbell (15)	173
Leonora Hanna (17)	174
Lauren Fitzpatrick (17)	174
Lauren Elder (15)	175
Diane Curran (14)	175
Steven Baird (13)	176
Jayne Annett (13)	176
Nicole Murphy (13)	177
Mark Burden (14)	177
Sara Russell (13)	178
Rebekah Campbell (13)	179
Natashia McCullough (15)	179
Christopher Maguire (12)	180
Diane Rooney (15)	180
Geoffrey McConnell (14)	180
Jemma McKee (12)	181
Stefan Johnston (13)	181
Samantha Woollard (12)	182
Alan Burden (13)	183
Kristofor Fitzpatrick (16)	183
Niall McMurray (16)	184
John Knox (15)	184
Andrew McCoy (15)	184
Zara Chambers (13)	185
Elaine Wackett (16)	185
Harold Robinson (13)	186
Michelle Burns (15)	186
Mark Annett (13)	186
Ricky Hanna (13)	187
Sarah-Jayne Annett (13)	187
Amy McKee (11)	188
Claire Annett (12)	188
Louise McConnell (12)	189
Judith Cherry (16)	190
Stacey Hanna (12)	190
Rachel Hanna (13)	191

Christopher Teggarty (13)	191
Rachel McConnell (14)	192
Samantha Hanna (13)	192
Philip Edgar (13)	193
Matthew Forsythe (13)	193
Chloe Johnston (14)	194
Leanne Hewitt (13)	194
Neil Stevenson (13)	195
Grace Scott (14)	195
Aimee Forsythe (13)	196
Jonathan Ewart (13)	196
Melissa Nicholson (13)	197
Jason McCulla (15)	197
Nathan Stewart (13)	198
Kelly Forsythe (15)	198
Dean McKee (11)	199
Andrew Patterson (13)	199
Alanna Fitzpatrick (12)	199
Andrew Charleton (11)	200
Lesley Ann Glenny (12)	200
Ryan Simpson (13)	201
Steven Cousins (14)	201
Vicky Wilson (13)	202
Adrian Annett (14)	202
Lisa Graham (14)	203
Nikki Scott (14)	203
Gary Johnston (12)	204
Matthew Hazard (12)	204
Alastair Parke (12)	205
David Hill (14)	205
Simon McKee (15)	206
Christopher Annett (13)	206
Karen Speers (15)	206
Mark Graham (15)	207
William Hanna (14)	207
Rebekah Heelham (13)	208
Melanie Newell (14)	208
Gregory McCullough (13)	209
Ruth Sloan (12)	209
Andrew Gordon (12)	210
Andrew Park (12)	210
Phillip Hanna (13)	210

Avril Edgar (17)	211
Gary Brown (11)	211
Adam Blakley (11)	212
Matthew Graham (13)	212
Rachel Haugh (11)	213
Laura-Jane Reilly (11)	213
Kathryn Edgar (14)	214
Colin Spence	214
Nicola Poole (17)	215
Lynda Annett (13)	216
Gregory Glenny (13)	216
Rachel Wackett (11)	217
William Gracey (14)	217
Daniel Smith (17)	218
Adrian Graham (13)	218
Rebekah Blue (12)	219
Andrew Cummins (14)	219
Jayne Scott (18)	220
Heather Speers (11)	220
Rachel Johnston (12)	221
William Poole (12)	221
Jade Lurring (12)	222
Orla Corbett (11)	222
Lindsey McConnell (17)	223
Gary Morris (13)	223
Stephen Gordon (12)	224
William Smyth (11)	224
Louise Houston (14)	225
Sarah McConnell (11)	225
Megan Wortley (12)	226
Anna Barbour (12)	226
Gareth Robinson (12)	227
Jessica Nugent (11)	227
Hannah Thompson (12)	228
Stacey Holmes (15)	228
Adele McConnell (12)	229
Simon Herron (12)	229
Thomas Nixon (14)	230

St Columbanus College, Bangor

Mauricia Croan (11)	230
Emma McColl (15)	231
Joanne Hamilton (15)	231
Leah Devanney (12)	232
Steven Rogan (15)	232
Matthew Morris (15)	233
Natalie McCloud (12)	233
Dominic McAvera (15)	234
Lynsey Reilly (16)	234
Merin D'cruz (12)	235
Leanne Smith (16)	235
Clare Houston (13)	236
Michael Brown (16)	237

St Malachy's High School, Castlewellan

Conor Boden (11)	237
Anna Brogan (11)	238
John Gallagher (11)	238
Rachel Dickson (11)	239
Rosemary O'Loughlin (12)	239
Rebecca McGreevy (12)	240
Gerard Corrigan (12)	240
Caoimhe Toner (12)	241
Roisin Malone (12)	241
Carol-Anne Magennis (11)	242

Strangford College

Andrew Dines (14)	242
Sarah Gregory (13)	243
Melissa Perkins (13)	243
Amanda Davies (14)	244
Ryan Fox (13)	244
Sabrina McCullough (13)	245
Leigh Savage (13)	245
Rebecca McKee (13)	246
Leeza Fitzsimmons (14)	246
Philip Wright (13)	247
Maria Waugh (13)	247
Samantha Townley (13)	248
Nikita Bewley (13)	248

Mikael Wilson (13)	249
Michael Braniff (14)	249
Andrew Danso (14)	250
Stephanie Gouldie (13)	250
Alannah Turner (13)	251
Jodie Dean (13)	252

The Poems

The Little Girl

She is stiff as a stone
Is it time for her to die?
Is it time for her spirit to leave her?
Will it fly on wings up high?

The little girl's not breathing,
She's drowning in the pool.
Will her parents soon be grieving?
Her father will call himself a fool.

We must do something
To save the little girl
My parents ran to the rescue
Her skin was white as a deep sea pearl.

Soon I heard a siren
Was she going to be OK?
Had the good Lord saved her
Or would this be her final day?

Slowly her eyes began to open
She came away from the light
And when I knew she was going to be fine
I felt as high as a kite.

Robert Crawford (13)
Abbey Grammar School

My Brother

My brother's from space,
He fits the profile no doubt,
He acts very strange.

He'll invade one day
With his followers and friends,
But when he does . . . *bang!*

I will shoot them all.
I will stop them in their tracks,
They won't come back here.

Colm Thompson (11)
Abbey Grammar School

Keano

My favourite footballer is Roy Keane
When he has the ball he's very mean.
He is always very hard
And maybe gets the odd red card!

He is good on the ball
And is as strong as a wall
In football he is tops
And when he runs he never stops!

He always gives his best
That's why he's better than the rest
And when he hits the ball a smack
The crowd goes up to clap, clap, clap!

When he retires, we'll all be sad
And for United it'll be very bad!

Niall McCartan (12)
Abbey Grammar School

Drip, Drop, Drip, Drop,

Drip, drop, drip, drop,
Go the raindrops,
Smack against the windowpane,
Driving me insane.

Waiting to go outside,
Energy building up inside,
But still the raindrops fall
And still no friends call.

Oh! Wait there's a light,
Oh drat!
It's only Mat's car light,
Still I wait, still inside.

Niall Daly (12)
Abbey Grammar School

Good Boy Jimmy

I once knew a boy called Jimmy,
He was as good as gold.
When I say this I mean he was never bold.
He went out to play with his friend one day,
That was Jimmy and his friend, Ray.

They played a game of rounders and had some fun
Then Jimmy hit it and he began to run.
Then suddenly came a big *crash!*
He hit a window and made it smash.

Ray's face went red, he then ran away.
Jimmy said, 'What will I do without Ray?'

Then came a man who began to say,
'Get that mess cleaned up today.'
Jimmy turned, he thought it was all
But then he said, 'Who owns this ball?'

Jimmy replied, 'It is mine!' and then he cried
That was the end of good boy Jimmy
And now he's not his mummy's honey.

Michael Courtney (12)
Abbey Grammar School

My Brother

My wee brother is small and stupid.
He's always messing with something.

He will run and run until he falls with a plop
And shouts, 'I want a bun!'

He will kick and scream if he wants something
And will not stop until he gets it,
He is as stubborn as a mule.

Turlough Tinnelly (13)
Abbey Grammar School

Young Writers - Great Minds From Co Down

The Little Old Man And His Little Old Dog

There was a little old man, who had a little old dog,
But his little old dog, fell in love with a little old frog.
The little old frog, was as green as a leaf
And all that it ate was steak, pork and beef.

The little old dog ran away from home,
So the little old man was left on his own.
The dog searched through rain, wind and fog,
Until eventually he found his darling green frog.

All was well in their little old den,
Until they both found out, that they were little old men!
The little old frog ran into the sea,
Splash! was the sound as the little frog drowned.

The little old dog decided to go home,
To his master he returned, again on his own.
The little old man was delighted to see
His little old dog, a shining face of glee.

Many long years they shared together,
Through the darkest storms and the brightest of weather.
Sadly both died, one scorching, sunny summer day,
The man and his dog on a soft pillow of hay.

J B Farrell (12)
Abbey Grammar School

White Hart Lane

The lane, the lane, White Hart Lane,
The sixties, the eighties, always the lane,
Nothing's as glorious as White Hart Lane.

Players like Brown, Baker and Greaves in the sixties,
Players like Jennings, Chivers and Peters in the seventies
And players now like Robinson, King, Defoe and Keane.

Goals, goals in White Hart Lane,
Goals in goal kicks, goals in free kicks
And Keane's skilful penalty kicks.

The lane has seen many good goals,
But Gazza's goal against Arsenal was the best,
A free kick, a free kick, a wonderful free kick!
Half-way line, as fast as a rocket and the keeper couldn't reach it.

The lane has seen many managers,
Bill Nicholson was the best,
The other team hadn't got time to rest,
Defending one second and sprinting forward the next.

So come on down to the lane,
See Ledley King tackle Wayne
And see the legends at their best.

Mathew Guy (12)
Abbey Grammar School

Clippety-Clop

As I walk down the country lane, I hear horses' hooves
Clippety-clop, clippety-clop, clippety-clop.
This is what tells me
The horses are on the move.

Pulling their carts, I hear them go,
Clippety-clop, clippety-clop, clippety-clop.
Most unlike the sound
They'd have made during snow.

Crash! Bang! Wallop! I hear the carts crash,
Clippety-clop, clippety-clop, clippety-clop, clippety-clop.
The horses start to run
Frightened by the smash.

'Whoa! Whoa!' I hear the farmer say,
Clippety-clop, the horses halt.
Tired by their run
They start to eat their hay.

Brendan Reid (13)
Abbey Grammar School

Silence

The night was so quiet
That the silence was there
In my back garden
It was so quiet
I could hear myself think!

The night was so quiet
That the sound of the air made my heart tremble
My ear, hearing something but nothing at all

The night was so quiet
That the sound of something came to my ear
I need to hear
Or I'll fear
The silence for evermore.

Cormac Clerkin Parr (13)
Abbey Grammar School

France

I went to a country called France
It is a great place.
Lovely country to stay in
For it has such an amount of space.

Hot, dry, sizzling sun
Brilliant space to be
Especially in the south
Beside the beautiful sea.

I have gone there so many times.
I really enjoyed it
I went to so many lovely places,
Never hated it a bit.

I really want to go back,
I had so much fun
Every time I go there
Great, brilliant, hot as the sun
In the country, France.

James Hasson (13)
Abbey Grammar School

The Corner

There is a corner in a room in my house,
Which is even too small for a mouse.
It creaks and breathes,
Like blowing leaves.
My brother and I are so full of fear,
So much that we never go near
That little corner.
But then one day I said,
'Today's the day, that I will go to the corner!'
So I got on my knees beside the corner,
Putting my head lower and lower,
Until I found out,
There was nothing in the corner!

Éoin Mulvaney (13)
Abbey Grammar School

Alton Towers

When my family and I reached Alton Towers,
Excitement took over me
I couldn't wait to get on the rides,
All the while yelling, 'Wheee!'

Although it was summer,
My ears were cold as ice
But when we entered the hotel
The warmth felt really nice.

After checking in we went to the park
Then I fell and whacked my face!
I was so sore I started saying silly words,
Blood was all over the place!

When we got to the ride, there was no line
And so we walked round the border
The man said, 'Folks, read the sign!'
And the blooming sign said, *Out of order!*

Adam Kane (12)
Abbey Grammar School

My School Trip

Up in the air for half an hour flight,
In through the window came a great light.

Down we descended oh what a sight!
I looked through the window and saw London up right.

I was so excited,
I nearly couldn't hide it.

We all had happy faces
And we visited some places.

We heard the shriek of a whistle,
It was like the sting of a thistle.

Alas it was time to go,
But did we want to, no!

Eoin Colgan (13)
Abbey Grammar School

Spirits Of The Graveyard

The silvery wind blew in the night,
Stay away from the graveyard or you're in for a fright,
I must admit it's a scary place
And if you come out there'll be no smirk on your face.

They say there are spirits lurking in the grounds,
Listen closely and you can hear strange sounds,
I must warn you not to go in,
Because with these spirits you'll never win.

The misty air is as cold as ice
And if you look carefully you can see some mice,
You may hear a dim clippety-clop,
But be aware you just might get the chop.

The rusty, red, ruined gates,
Are there for the safety of you and your mates,
Get out, get out or you might just find,
That these spirits have the power to take over your mind!

Dermot Markey (12)
Abbey Grammar School

Old Drew - Haikus

Old Drew is scary,
He is very old and cool,
Dangerous Old Drew.

His hair is grey and
His eyes are very evil,
His face is wrinkled.

He lives in Newtown
And chases all the women
And they run away.

He wears a big coat,
He is very, very fat,
An alcoholic.

Matthew Small (11)
Abbey Grammar School

George Best

George Best is simply the best
Better than all the rest.
When he has the ball
He's sure to dazzle the defender and make him fall.

When he has the ball
He takes on defenders big and small,
Then he has a shot with the ball
To have a two-all draw.

How much does he get paid?
That's all everyone said,
He's sure to get a lot
For all the skills he displays.

When he dropped with a severe knee injury,
He knew that it was time for him to stop.
But that didn't stop George from
Being simply the best.

Patrick Quinn (13)
Abbey Grammar School

Windy Wind

The night was so windy
That a whisper came through the trees
And the branches of a tree were waiting to
Snap!

The night was so windy
That a breeze filled the cold, crisp air
And made your teeth
Chatter!

The night was so windy
That a *whoosh!*
Filled the trees
Now the wind turned, still
And Ireland won 1-0.

Paul McShane (12)
Abbey Grammar School

Haunted House

There's a house upon the hilltop
We will not go inside
For that is where the witches live,
Where ghosts and goblins hide.

Tonight they have their party,
All the lights are burning bright,
But we will not dare go inside
The haunted house tonight.

The demons they are whirling
And the spirits swirl about.
They sing their songs to Hallowe'en.
'Hallowe'en night will give you such a fright,'
They shout.

But we do not dare to go there
So we run with all our might
We will not go inside
The haunted house tonight.

Ethan Toner (13)
Abbey Grammar School

My Best Friend

My best friend's kind of cool,
He never works in school.
My other friends think he's a geek,
No, he's just a bit weak.

He's as big as a bear,
He'd give you a stare.
He's got funny hair,
But he's always there.

He helps you out,
And gives you a shout.
I don't think I would attend,
Without my best friend.

Ryan Quigg (12)
Abbey Grammar School

Young Writers - Great Minds From Co Down

Witches And Wizards

Witches and wizards they fly
About all night.
Witches and wizards they
Will give you a fright.

Witches with brooms,
Witches with wands,
They could turn you to stone,
As each day dawns.

Wizards do tricks,
Witches do spells.
If you don't abide with them,
They will banish you to Hell.

Witches can be evil,
Wizards can be too.
Stay indoors at Hallowe'en,
For they might just get to you.

Jack McShane (12)
Abbey Grammar School

My Friend Tom

My friend Tom is like a time bomb!
Everywhere we go, you think he's going to blow!
When we play football he always shouts!
Taking the ball and messing about.

Sometimes I pretend he's not my friend!
Probably because he drives me round the bend.
I think he's mad, so does my dad
Luckily he's not my only friend - I should be glad!

Playing on the streets he's really bad
He's not very nice but you should see his dad!
Now that he's grown up he's had a change
But still he's very strange!

Ciaran McEvoy (12)
Abbey Grammar School

Glory, Glory!

Even non-supporters would marvel at the sight,
Old Trafford's glory and the fans' delight.
The derby games are so much fun,
We have Man City on the run.

Seated in the Stretford End,
We pray this day will never end.
The floodlights see the pitch alight,
So we can see the Devils fight.

Arsenal are having great craic,
But now we want our title back.
The Gunners will howl in pain,
For we will be the champs again.

The Champions League is for the taking,
The old United in the making.
We will also win the FA Cup,
As the Reds go marching *up!*

Michael Beswick (13)
Abbey Grammar School

My Friend

Ever since I was two,
My friend Cathal
Has known me through and through.

In our school days we were best of mates,
When classes started we were always late,
When the football started we were great,
The opposing team were always beat.

Odd times we got into rows,
Which the teacher never allowed.
Now we are in different schools,
Which isn't cool.

Now we don't see each other much,
But at least we get to see each other as such.

Colum Gildea (12)
Abbey Grammar School

Young Writers - Great Minds From Co Down

Alone

Alone in the house
Not a sound to be heard.
It's hard to admit but I'm kind of scared.

Nobody to talk to
Everyone's away.
The sun has gone down
It's the end of the day.

No music to play,
Nothing is on TV
And I can't help but think
Is someone watching me?

In the midst
Black shadows move and twist
Watching, waiting
Wondering what's out there.

Out of the shadows
As quick as a flash
My cat runs out,
I watch her dash.

I let her in
She jumps on my lap
Now, I'm not so alone.

Michael Vallely (13)
Abbey Grammar School

Racing Days

He smiled contentedly
As he thought of
His younger days.
He had a full and
Happy life.
He closed his
Eyes and
Drifted into
The past.

Off went the hare
The traps went up
And the race was on!
Oh the thrill of it.
His heart beating like a drum.
The elation when he won.

Celebrating afterwards
A laugh and a joke
Sarcasm and frowning
From some folk.
Travelling home with
Family and friends.
Oh what a joyous end.

Christopher Quinn (12)
Abbey Grammar School

Paris

So magnificent in sight,
It's such a delight.
The tower sprouts up,
From the city below.
The lights flicker and flash,
A beautiful glow.
I stand in awe,
Observing the comings and
Goings around me.

Twin towers so tall and square,
Shoot up high in the air.
The bells ring aloud,
Ding, ding, ding!
Calling the flock to the cathedral
On the island.

Busy, busy, busy,
Dizzy, dizzy, dizzy.
So mighty, so tall,
Ever so great,
Standing like a mammoth gate.
In the middle of Paris
It stands so proud,
Traffic around it,
Ever so loud.
Like a herd of elephants
In the jungle wild.

Gazing at the museum,
With its cold water fountains,
Rivers of gold and pyramid mountains,
The beauty outside,
Hides the beauty within.

Never to be sold,
Among paintings of old.
It's worth it to wait a while,
To see the Mona Lisa smile.

Daniel McCormick (12)
Abbey Grammar School

Stephen Gerrard

Gerrard is my hero
My idol through and through
His tackles as fierce as a lion
His runs as fast as a tiger
He's so good he'd put you in a rigor!

He gets the ball from Cisse
He dribbles here and there
He forwards as quick as lightning
Bang! The ball is in the net!
And oh how he made me win that bet!

He runs along the sideline
Doing cartwheels as he goes
We all shout and shake our rattles
He gives a cheer to the crowd
As he returns back to the battle!

It's the final score,
Even though we shout for more!
Gerrard! Gerrard my hero
Through and through!

Sean McDonnell (12)
Abbey Grammar School

Run From A Gun

There is an old man who lives up my way,
Who doesn't like it when we noisily play,
A game of football in our street every day.

He sometimes comes out,
And often he shouts,
But still we noisily play
Football every day.

But one day when he came out,
We knew what it was about,
He was carrying a gun,
So we started to run,
Like a greyhound would run,
Away from our street,
Never to play,
Football in our street, anymore, any day.

Tony Fearon (13)
Abbey Grammar School

Quiet!

The night was so quiet,
That the buzz of the lamp,
Came to my ear.
A headache thumping
To get out!

The night was so quiet,
That the breeze in the trees,
Came to my ear,
Like the whispers of a mouse
Lost in a maze.

The night was so quiet,
That the quiet of the quietness,
Came to my ear,
Like the drum of my ear
Deaf!

Oliver Hearty (13)
Abbey Grammar School

Young Writers - Great Minds From Co Down

My Friend, The Parrot

My friend is like a parrot,
His nose is like a beak,
To him I am a monkey,
Lazing in the heat.

Imagine my friend squawking,
The whole way through the day,
Imagine my friend talking,
Repeating everything you say.

When I call him parrot,
He squawks right back at me,
'Hey, massive moaning monkey,
Go and climb a tree.'

I shout out loud and say,
'I'd rather be an ape,
Climbing trees throughout the day,
Than be a dumb recording tape.'

Sean Fegan (12)
Abbey Grammar School

My Dog

My dog is nice and small,
She looks just like a fox,
She is meant to be a house dog,
And will never sleep in her box.

She runs about the garden,
Barking loud and mad,
When she falls and hurts herself,
It is rather sad.

You now know what my dog is like,
Did I mention her name?
It is quite silly for a dog,
That she is called Jane!

Ryan Devlin (12)
Abbey Grammar School

Young Writers - Great Minds From Co Down

They're So Bad - Haikus

This team is awful
They're absolutely awful
They're losing ten-nil.

Roar, go all their fans
But I don't know how they could
Support *The Rangers.*

They're losing by twelve
Two goals in seven minutes
What a big surprise!

They shoot like those cows
I'm surprised they can kick balls.
There's another goal!

Thirteen to nothing
Almost the football record . . .
Of losing a match!

Ten minutes are left
Until the match is over.
Seventeen-nothing.

The Celts are away . . .
Petrov shoots, the world record
Has just been broken!

The former record
Seventeen goals to nothing
Now *eighteen to none!*

Aodhan Byrne (11)
Abbey Grammar School

What A Desperate Day

The coach door opened,
Just there I stood,
Full of excitement,
Like a balloon ready to burst.

I looked at the sign,
This read *Lisburn Leisure Centre,*
I couldn't wait so I stepped up the pace,
But thirty others had won the race.

I took my place in the queue,
It wasn't long before I was going through,
I hurried in and got changed,
Before long I was on my way.

I rushed out the door and
Looked around, I saw,
Huge, slippery, slimy slides and diving boards,
It felt like receiving an adventurous all-star award.

I ran towards a slide,
But I didn't see the step,
Then suddenly I fell, my ankle went,
It felt like the clanging of a bell.

Next thing I knew,
I was lying on the chair,
All I could say was,
What a desperate day.

Sean McMahon (13)
Abbey Grammar School

My Baby Brother

His name is Dara
And he's nine months old,
He's the best thing since sliced pan
Or so I've been told.

He sits in his high chair
He sleeps in his cot
And when he wants attention
He just cries a lot.

My parents make a fuss of him
And smile at him with glee,
Looking, laughing, loving
Leaving little time for me.

They thought he was a clever clogs
When he said, 'Wa, wa, wa,'
Now he's a gifted genius
'Cause he said, 'Da, da, da.'

His future lies ahead of him
All planned out by his mother,
But when he gets a bit of sense
He'll look up to his brother.

Owen Carragher (12)
Abbey Grammar School

What A Day In Croke Park

The ball was thrown in,
The battle began,
As Ireland looked for the win.
Mattie Forde collected the ball,
We all knew it was in.

Cavanagh was strong,
It went in the net
And left Australia in the wrong.
Half-time blew,
The Irish crew withdrew.

Second half had begun,
McDonald prepared to run,
He collected the ball,
And delighted us all,
As the ball was in the back of the net.

The whistle blew,
Ireland had won,
We knew that next week,
Would be the big one.

Michael McKevitt (12)
Abbey Grammar School

Christmas Day

Malachy had a very hard life
It was full of torture and grief
His father died, his sister too
His grandparents, from the flu

Then one faithful day
His ship sailed out
To the shores of great England
But on his doorstep he made a solemn vow
That he would come back and see his mother
Somehow

But little did he know
Because of drink
He wouldn't get home
No matter what he would think

But one night in Jack Smith's pub
The barmaid came over and said,
'Hey bub, are you not going home for Christmas Day?'
He shook his head and said, 'No way.'
He told her the story of his life
There and then he made a promise
That he would go home and give his mother a kiss

So he picked up all the money that he could find
Even in the dirt and grind
Then he got on the gigantic boat
Left the harbour and set afloat
But as the captain he knew well from home
Heard him say, 'At least I'll be home for Christmas Day,'
Told him the story of the previous day,
'No doctor or pill could cure your mother
It had been sent in a letter from your brother
She died yesterday
The funeral is after Mass
On Christmas Day.'

Conor Murtagh (13)
Abbey Grammar School

Little Boy

Small and mischievous, alert for fun
This little boy like the wind can run.
Out to play, his work for the day
Tall as a tower,
Blowing like a flower,
Racing like a car,
He has ultimate power.

Boundless energy,
Like a fully charged battery.
Jumping fences
Hitting knees
Scoring goals
He's very pleased!

Bedtime begs, tired and weary
He trudges home, his day well spent
Happy and content,
He falls in a heap,
Little boy is ready to sleep.

Steven Fearon (12)
Abbey Grammar School

I'll See You Soon

I remember my granda
Lying on his deathbed
The thoughts going through my head.
'I have to leave you,' he cried,
With a sparkle in his eye.
A tear ran down my cheek
I knew he was going to die.
He caught the tear in his huge, hairy hand,
He breathed his last breath
And then I witnessed his death.
When he died I was only eleven.
But I'll see him again some day
In Heaven.

David Hudson (13)
Abbey Grammar School

Young Writers - Great Minds From Co Down

My Big, Fat Aunty Ann

My big, fat aunty Ann raps the door like a drum
And when she sits, she breaks the chairs with her full moon bum!

The clatter and banging of cups makes her go crazy,
I tell her to lose weight but she's way too lazy!

Once she's finished her twenty or so buns,
She attempts to eat her million and one crumbs!

She's never any good for chat,
I try to sneak off because she's as blind as a bat!

My mum always tells her to exercise,
But I know, that her slimy, sweaty skin attracts flies!

When she slams the door goodbye,
I think, *phew, for once she didn't eat the last steak pie!*

Finally, I decided to cut her some slack,
But then to my horror, she came back!

Patrick Gallogly (12)
Abbey Grammar School

Robbie Keane - Haikus

He scores goals for Spurs,
He scores goals for Ireland too.
Celebrates in style!

He dribbles past one,
He is as fast as lightning.
The crowd chant and cheer.

Have you seen him roll?
Everybody shouts Keano!
He is our hero.

He is amazing,
Future king of all Ireland.
He is Robbie Keane.

Sean McCaffery (12)
Abbey Grammar School

What A Loss!

Mr Pat Mooney was like a car,
Start him up and you'd go far,

'Books out!'
He would yell,
But the anger then soon fell.

Fun with him was so true
It was like a kid in the zoo.

Time would pass,
Till the bell would go,

Ding-a-ling-a-ling,
'Oh no!'

'See you soon lads,'
Said his sacred soul,
Leaving there a hole,
Where we would go!

Ryan Hudson (13)
Abbey Grammar School

The Mountains - Haikus

Towering over
The smaller hills, as tall as
The sky, reaching the

Clouds, making mere mounds,
Melt with envy they wish to
Be up there looking

Down on ev'ryone
Else, to be the biggest of
Them all. Up there they

See everything
And ev'ryone, they can hear
Wind, they are mountains.

Owen Jones (11)
Abbey Grammar School

My Auntie - Haikus

My auntie is great,
You can't get better than her,
She loves the children.

She is great at work,
She's as fit as a fiddle,
She's very helpful.

You can't catch her out.
She is as wise as an owl,
Bang! She cracks puzzles!

She plays the organ
And conducts the church choir
And never drinks wine.

After all I've said,
The amazing thing is that,
She is eighty-two!

Stephen Doherty (11)
Abbey Grammar School

The President - Haikus

The name is George Bush
Ruler of America
Top of everyone.

I'm the best at war
I'm the best at everything
Yet no one likes me.

But I wonder why
I'm cool aren't I? Yes I am!
I'm top of the vote!

That old John Kerry
He thinks he is the hero
But vote me, George Bush!

Oisin McGuinness (11)
Abbey Grammar School

Paris - Haikus

I'm off to Paris
Tomorrow morning, airport!
Off with Thomas Cook

Croissants and coffee
My favourite breakfast food
My delight - Paris!

The Eiffel Tower
The Arc De Triomphe is great
The secret soldier!

I'm off to Ireland
It is my favourite place
Delightful Ireland!

Paris is lovely
But Ireland is really best
I'll stay here always!

Kevin Gribben (12)
Abbey Grammar School

My Dad - Haikus

My dad is the one
Who wears that blue baseball hat
And shouts at the ref!

My dad is the one
Who went to St Colman's school
Which is number two!

My dad is the one
With hair as grey as cement
Which used to be blonde!

My dad is the one
Who was born in Lurgan town
Gerard is his name.

Oisín Lynch (11)
Abbey Grammar School

Young Writers - Great Minds From Co Down

Anfield - Haikus

He's got it surely
He takes it down on his chest
He shoots . . . hits the bar!

The crowd are in tears
And the ball bounces back out
He goes to rebound

Bang, it's surely in!
It hits the defender's hand
The ref blows it up

As loud as a bomb
Who's taking it? they wonder
Milan Baros will

He sets the ball down,
Looks up to the sunny sky
And then he shoots. *Bang!*

Yes! It's in the net
Liverpool have won the match
Anfield has gone wild.

Glenn McConville (12)
Abbey Grammar School

The Hero - Haikus

He is the hero
He plays for *Armagh* seniors
And scores loads of goals

Takes the penalties
And never has missed one yet
He takes points as well

Plays in full-forward
He sets up a lot of goals
Runs fast as the wind

Finally the day
Playing in the All-Ireland
Taking the points well

Then the best chance came
He missed the penalty, was
So devastated

Then fifteen minutes
The goal comes by the hero
It is all over!

Patrick McConville (12)
Abbey Grammar School

Andrew Lloyd Webber - Haikus

Haunts the opera,
Phantom Of The Opera,
Wearing his great mask.

Argentina weeps,
Only for great Evita,
Cried ever so long.

They give you a purr,
It is the amazing Cats,
They are the prowlers.

We pray to you God,
It's Jesus Christ Superstar,
You have answered us.

Andrew Lloyd Webber,
Thanks for all your great music,
It is a delight.

Rory Devlin (11)
Abbey Grammar School

Cristiano Ronaldo - Haikus

He twists and dodges,
Just like a slippery eel,
Keep an eye on him!

He dances and jives,
In the crowd, we hear his name,
He feints like a ghost!

His skills are unique,
He's a master of his craft,
He is magical.

Wears number seven,
Seventeen for his country,
He is Ronaldo.

Rory Keenan (11)
Abbey Grammar School

The Desert Nightmare - Haikus

Can't believe I'm here
Hatred heat's unbearable
Will I survive this?

My mouth is parching
Wait! Hold on is that a well?
Run towards it now!

Wait! Where did it go?
This place is as dry as sand
That's what it is - sand!

There is a green plant
And there's some - wait, what is it?
It's that gusting wind?

The wind it goes swish!
There's a pointy pyramid
Suddenly I wake.

Garbhan McKevitt (12)
Abbey Grammar School

Old Trafford - Haikus

The best team has the
Seventy-two thousand fans
Cheering go Man U!

Big money was put
To building the stadium
Was named Old Trafford!

The fans dressed in red
Shouting go, go, go!
Cheering champions!

Beating Arsenal
By four goals to none or one
What a lovely game!

Scott Gray (11)
Abbey Grammar School

Young Writers - Great Minds From Co Down

The Mysterious Man - Haikus

My dad said there's an
Extraordinary man
That lives in a cave!

My dad says he is
A very talented man.
He stands on his head?

My dad saw and said
That he eats nothing a-day
And he never sleeps?

Now every day
I do wonder who he is
But never find out.

Liam Gray (11)
Abbey Grammar School

Pirate's Cove - Haikus

Skull and crossbones there,
Go take a look if you dare,
Buried treasure found.

Walk across bridges,
Water gushes out with force,
Splash! Wet as a fish.

Eye-patches, daggers,
People like pirates pillage,
Murderous sea dogs.

Dark caves and caverns,
Many tunnels to go through,
Do not lose your way.

On this course of fun,
Crazy golf has to be won,
Down the hole in one!

Kevin Quinn (11)
Abbey Grammar School

Florida - Haikus

Bang went the thunder
Ev'ryone ran for shelter
Out of the hard rain

After, so sunny
Bright and cheerful all will be
As bright as the sun

So big, brilliant
It's as much fun as swimming
So hot and rainy

Disneyland, what fun
All the fun of the fair there
Lots to do and see!

A long way from home
All aboard the big jet plane
It's time for some sleep!

Conor Carroll (11)
Abbey Grammar School

Roy Keane - Haikus

Roy Keane is pure class
His hair is as black as coal
Shirt as green as grass

Roy Keane is pure class
The mighty, mean, man from Cork
Who'd dare to provoke

Roy Keane is pure class
He's our hero of the green
He has got it all

Roy Keane is pure class
Skill, speed, now we hear them chant!
Go for it Keano!

Conor McKinley (12)
Abbey Grammar School

Who Is This? - Haikus

There was an old man
With a long, snowy, white beard
With twelve great big pets

A very nice man
Who owns a toy company
And gives out free toys

His wife is nice too
But she doesn't have a beard
She likes children lots

He wears a big coat
And it's coloured red and white
The same as his hat

Once a year at night
He goes away with his pets
To deliver toys

He's been here for years
And will be here for lots more
He is Santa Claus.

Cian Gallagher (12)
Abbey Grammar School

Me And My Animals - Haikus

Hi, my name is James
I have real strange animals
I'll explain them all.

Freddie the frog-man
Half man and also half frog
Can jump very high.

Kruger the huge cat
With five-centimetre claws
Could slice you in two.

Lightning the turtle
Can run as fast as a lynx
And he never tires.

Frank the magic fish
Grants me any wish I want
And will never die.

Now I've wakened up
I have had my Sugar Puffs
And I'm off to school.

James Morgan (12)
Abbey Grammar School

The Lady Of The Night - Haikus

She hides in her cave
With long hair as black as coal
Many secrets held.

Delights on her broom
Flying high in the dark sky
She hovers around.

Black cat by her side
Screeching and lamenting fright
Evil in her eyes.

She brings fear to all
With her potions and her spells
Darkness is her joy.

She stirs her cauldron
While she cackles to herself
Hallowe'en has come . . .

Martin Hearty (11)
Abbey Grammar School

My Sister - Haikus

My scary sister
Her evil eyes burn my skin
Eyes as red as fire.

I scream and I run
But she will always find me
She comes closer.

She has got me now
Bang! I am dragged out, bang!
I can see darkness.

Slowly I wake up
It is as dark as coal out
It was all a dream!

Peter Hollowood (11)
Abbey Grammar School

My Brother - Haikus

My moaning brother
Is very, very bossy
He is annoying!

I have to tidy
When he messes the house up
I clean everything!

He always blames me
He's evil like the Devil
He breaks all my toys!

He never does work
He wrecks my room all the time
He thinks he is cool.

If I'm looking bored
He will play football with me
He is good at golf.

Daniel McCullagh (11)
Abbey Grammar School

Fireworks - Haikus

It's tiny and light
With a destructive small fuse
It is just fireworks!

The fireworks are bright,
Colourful, sparkly and they
Have a rocket's boom!

They light up the sky
With a nice, attractive, big
And romantic scene.

Fireworks can be used
At Hallowe'en for the crack
For the children's fun!

Fergal McEvoy (11)
Abbey Grammar School

Old Man Bob - Haikus

There is an old man,
Who lives on our street named Bob,
He's a war hero.

As bold as brass he
Went to the war with a knife
Killed thousands with it.

All he does now is
Moan and groan about his wife
She had died last year.

They're taking Bob to
A home tomorrow, bye-bye
Bob we'll miss you lots.

We'll remember you
In years and years with tales of
The old war days too.

Christopher Fearon (12)
Abbey Grammar School

Africa - Haikus

The wide open plains,
The country of Africa,
Animals roam wild.

Animals watching,
Birds soaring, swooping, diving,
Thunderous stampede!

Sunny skies darken,
The animals take a rest
Till another day.

Natives sit and watch
Near the glow of warming fires,
Feast on their day's kill.

Colum Mackey (12)
Abbey Grammar School

Homer - Haikus

Bald as an eagle,
Yellow as a canary,
His catchphrase is, 'Doh!'

Drinks in Moe's Tavern
With pals Barney and Lennie,
Getting drunk on Duff.

Gurgling saliva,
Feeding his fat, round belly,
On Dunkin' donuts.

When Bart is naughty,
He throttles his neck tightly
And threatens to kill.

Homer, our hero
From old Evergreen Terrace,
With stories to tell!

Patrick Burns (11)
Abbey Grammar School

Bundoran - Haikus

Bundoran busy
Flashing slot machines surround
Coins flowing out fast!

Bundoran beach, wet
Seashells, pebbles all around
Crashing waves foaming.

Bundoran parks full
Laughing children playing games
Mums watching sternly.

Bundoran pubs sing
Brown ale and spirits ordered
Home time comes too soon.

Matthew McGivern (11)
Abbey Grammar School

London's Eye - Haikus

The London Eye is
Big or small or very tall,
Which one could it be?

I think it is large,
As large as it could ever
Be! Small, tall maybe?

It looks over me
And maybe *ev'ryone* in
London, London Eye.

Big or small, who cares?
Not me, do you? So why is
The London Eye big?

Tick-tock, tick-tock, tick
It stops there because it's a
Big, big watchtower.

Deaglan O'Neill (12)
Abbey Grammar School

My Dear Old Grandpa! - Haikus

My dear old grandpa,
He smokes like an old steam train,
He just loves to smoke!

My dear old grandpa
Wears woolly socks tucked into
His green welly boots!

My dear old grandpa
Has some very bad habits,
Spitting, kicking me!

I love him so much,
My dearest, grumpy grandpa
Is so dear to me!

James O'Gorman (11)
Abbey Grammar School

It's Fatso!

A butt ugly face,
Like the goblin from
The Lord of the Rings!

He looks like a huge,
Disgusting woolly mammoth,
When his top is off!

Error will appear
On the scales because Fatso
Weighs six hundred pounds!

His son is *Bam!* and
His brother is Don Vito.
His wife is April!

Have you got it yet?
Go, try and guess who it is.
It's Phil Margera!

Gavin O'Hare (11)
Abbey Grammar School

Bam Margera - Haikus

A black Him Beanie,
Ragged jeans ripped at the hem,
Pink, Powell T-shirt.

Friends with Tony Hawk,
He's sponsored by Element,
Serious skater.

Heart tattoo on wrist,
Heartagram print on stomach,
Crazy man on arm.

Fourteen set of steps,
Double kickflip, bang, landed,
Like a ton of bricks.

David Morgan (12)
Abbey Grammar School

The Guy I Met - Haikus

I met this boy, his
Name was Josh, he seemed OK
At the time we met.

But that night I heard
A voice saying something I
Could not hear at first.

Out of the distance
A white man approached and said
Josh died a while back.

The man disappeared
And I went back to sleep, the
Next day I saw Josh.

It was scary 'cause
It looked like he had no legs
Then he ran away.

Ryan O'Hare (11)
Abbey Grammar School

Armagh! - Haikus

Armagh have won it
Joe Kernan's like a rocket,
Waiting to explode.

Stevie's on a role,
He scores lots of points and goals,
Whizzing and whirling.

Cooper and O'Shea
Had nearly Sam in their grasp,
But stopped by Armagh.

Armagh have done it
With Stevie and McGeeney,
Sam is comin' home!

Conor McVeigh (11)
Abbey Grammar School

The Place - Haikus

People come and go,
But this place is mystic too,
People who see it.

There are rivers there
That are adjacent to my
Lovely perfect place.

This place is such fun
The ducks go splash in the pond
This place is secret.

Others call it weird
Some call it fantastic but
I think it's neither.

Then there are those caves
Which are as cold as ice if
People come and go.

Brian Comaskey (11)
Abbey Grammar School

Kilkenny - Haikus

Kilkenny is the
Best place in the whole of Earth
With DJ Carey.

I like Kilkenny
Because it started hurling
And it's really cool!

Kilkenny is the
Best except for Warrenpoint
Which rules all the land!

I think Warrenpoint
Is the better town indeed
But Kilkenny rules.

Jason Gray (11)
Abbey Grammar School

My Dad - Haikus

Is definitely
Coolest dad in the whole world,
He drives a cool car.

He loves my mum and
Also loves me, that's my dad,
The best dad ever.

He loves football too,
We always watch the matches
Together, just us.

And if we score we
Shout so loud that our neighbours
Can hear us those nights!

If something breaks and
Makes a *bang!* he'll know who it
Was, he'll know it's me!

Mark Rocks (12)
Abbey Grammar School

Thierry Henry - Haikus

Thierry is class
He is better than Pele
He is so superb.

He's a joy to watch
He can skin ev'rybody
He's simply the best.

He plays for a team
The best team in the country
Nicknamed the Gunners.

He's getting a Merc'
So it says on the tele,
He is really rich!

Stephen O'Hare (11)
Abbey Grammar School

My Mum! - Haikus

She cooks the dinner
As fast as a cheetah and
Sizzles on the pan.

She makes the bed and
Washes the sheets, shrieking when
Dirt does not come out!

She cleans the clothes and
Like a floor cleaner, rubs, rubs
At them until clean.

Why does she do these
Things? I ask myself, just why
Does she do these things?

Dermot McVeigh (12)
Abbey Grammar School

Mr

Comin' down the street
Blood is dripping down his skull,
People are screaming.

Looking at the house
Where he died as a young boy
Screeching, no, no, no!

Standing there with a
Sharp knife in his hand roaring
No! No! No! No! No!

He turns round again
And runs at us . . . and someone
Falls . . . Stab, stab, blood pours!

Jordan Havern (11)
Abbey Grammar School

Young Writers - Great Minds From Co Down

Tenerife - Haikus

Tenerife is cool,
I love to swim in the sea
Though the sand is black.

Paddling and swimming,
Chasing and splashing big sis,
Boating in sunshine.

Loro Parque, parrots,
Penguins, African dancers,
Seals and sea lions.

The water park slides,
My first jump off the high board
And hot, so hot sun.

John-Joe Aitken (11)
Abbey Grammar School

Football Field - Haikus

Brown passes the ball
Misses and falls in a heap
Blew his only chance!

But never gave up
Ryan tried again for goal
And this time he scored!

The team was happy
Especially Ryan Giggs
And the fans cheered him!

He was interviewed
And Ryan was made captain
He was delighted!

Rory Devlin (12)
Abbey Grammar School

Cheetah

The cheetah creeps
Slowly into the deep
Grass stealthily, suddenly
The cheetah springs out
Of the grass with the
Muscles bulging. Swiftly
And professionally the
Cheetah catches the prey
And tears it apart with
Powerful jaws and with
A horrid grin.

Daniel Campbell (14)
Ardmore House Special School

My Granny

My granny is so good,
My granny I love her to bits,
My granny treats me to things,
My granny cooks the dinner,
My granny gives me money.
She has brown hair, she is skinny and very old,
Sometimes she can moan, but I always forgive her.
She always gets very lonely, but I'm always there for my granny.
I don't know what I'd do without my very old granny.

Tina Mairs (18)
Clifton Special School

I Love Singing

My name is James, I love to sing,
100 songs I know
And most of all I love to sing
Beside the piano.

In school I sing in music class
On Thursday afternoon.
'Mellow The Moonlight To Shine Is Beginning',
Is a very lovely tune.

At home I always sing along
To my Daniel O'Donnell CD.
'There's Always A Fire In The Kitchen',
Is just the one for me!

I like to sing to Boyzone,
I sometimes dance along.
'Love Me For A Reason',
Is my other favourite song.

I like the Nolan's singing,
I think they're very good.
'I'm In The Mood For Dancing',
Puts me in a happy mood.

I'll maybe join the school choir
Or play in our school band,
But singing for my friends in class
Is really just as grand!

James Skelton (17)
Clifton Special School

My Music

My name is Kathy Galway
And I am seventeen.
I like to listen to music,
I also like to sing.

At home I play my CDs,
I play them in my room.
I use my new Pop Idol
Karaoke machine.

I'm good at singing to Eminem,
It puts me in a good mood,
But some songs I wouldn't sing in school
Because the words are rude.

I play the music up loud
And sing along with him.
Sometimes Mum says, 'Turn that down,
That noise is doing my head in.'

My very favourite music
Is my Barbie Girl CD,
I shout and sing along with it
Like I am on TV.

In school I like our music class,
We've lots of songs to sing.
The one that I like best is called,
'Hosanna the King of Kings'.

Kathy Galway (17)
Clifton Special School

My Cat Jasper

My cat is called Jasper and he says miaow!
He is black.
Every morning, afternoon and night
He keeps on eating and eating and eating.
He miaows and he miaows for his dinner.
He comes to the front door and he miaows!
Then he comes to the back door and he miaows!
Jasper wants to get inside. Sometimes he sits outside the window,
Then he starts to miaow!
When he wants to go outside, he starts messing about.
He jumps on the chairs, on the telephone table.
He jumps on the pool table, the beds, and the kitchen table
And the living room sofas, the dining room table and chairs.
Sometimes he sleeps on the sofa or the floor and beds.
In the kitchen I open the fridge or freezer,
Jasper looks inside and smells things in it.
He's looking for food again.

Dave Gordon (16)
Clifton Special School

Levi

My dog is called Levi,
He's not a pair of jeans,
He's a cuddly little poodle,
But boy can he bite.
If he doesn't get his way
Then you won't get yours.
He's the boss of the house
Though he's only one foot tall.

Robyn Loyer (16)
Clifton Special School

Football

My favourite team is Man United,
They are the Red Devils,
Their kit is red and white.
The players all kick, pass and shoot,
Put the ball in the net - it's a goal!
It is a goal, a very good goal!
Man United score and win the Cup,
The football cup is coming *home*,
Home to Man United's Old Trafford.

David Morton (16)
Clifton Special School

Holly's Recipe For Happiness

(Inspired by 'Recipe for Happiness' by Hugh Clement)

A good ounce of going to the cinema on a Saturday morning
With a scoop of presents and a splash of videos.
Stir up well with a large spoonful of music,
Pour in some holidays and a good cup of swimming,
Covered with a Christmas or two.
Add in some drawings and a good long cycle,
In goes an hour of fun in the garden.
Sprinkle in some Easter eggs
And some yummy sweets.
Add a sprinkle of going to the beach
And serve with a good long weekend of fun!

Holly Chambers (11)
Glastry High School

Graeme's Recipe For Happiness

(Inspired by 'Recipe for Happiness' by Hugh Clement)

A gram of bed,
Mixed with swimming,
Stirred with some rugby,
Beat up with some TV,
Add a pinch of quads,
Cut up with woodwork,
Bake well with movies,
Cut up some dogs,
An ounce of pizza,
Serve with PlayStation 2,
And eat up.

Graeme Warden (12)
Glastry High School

Junita's Recipe For Happiness

(Inspired by 'Recipe for Happiness' by Hugh Clement)

A slice of TV then . . .
Add a pinch of shopping,
Next add a lump of seeing my dad,
Mix it up well,
Then add a tablespoon of chocolate.
Next add a jar of money,
Then add a kilo of trampolining,
Add a gram of music.
Next add a spoonful of games
And there you are the recipe's done.

Junita Coffey (11)
Glastry High School

My Recipe For Happiness

(Inspired by 'Recipe for Happiness' by Hugh Clement)

Pour in a jar of shopping with my friends,
A sprinkle of school with my friends,
A gram of listening to music,
Mix in a heap of reading books,
Chop in a kilogram of watching TV,
Stir in a glass of going on holiday,
Mash a bag of riding my bike,
Sprinkle in a spoonful of having friends down,
Bake it in with a bit of singing
And serve it with a sprinkle of family and friends.

Hazel Montgomery (12)
Glastry High School

Kirsty's Recipe For Happiness

(Inspired by 'Recipe for Happiness' by Hugh Clement)

Mix up an hour of playing with friends,
Stir in a tablespoon of listening to music,
Add a slice of singing,
Pour in some shopping,
Sprinkle in some watching movies,
Add half a cup of reading magazines,
Mash in a little bit of eating sweets,
Squeeze in a little bit of games,
Pour in a jar of playing the dance mat
And beat in watching the music channels
And that's my recipe for happiness.

Kirsty Mills (12)
Glastry High School

My First Day At Big School

On my first day at big school
I was quite nervous, but excited.
My mum made sure I had everything
And then took me to my bus stop.
I waited for my bus
And when it came I had my bus pass ready.
'Bus pass please,' the driver said,
I showed him my pass.
I had to stand because there were no seats left,
Though I didn't mind.
When we got to school my mind was racing,
I met up with my friend and we headed in.
We found out our classes then met our group tutor,
We stayed in the same class all day
And talked about the school.
We got to go home at 12 o'clock,
I got the bus home.
When I got home my mum asked,
'How was your day?'
'Excellent,' I said.
That was my first day at big school!

Rebecka McCormick (11)
Glastry High School

All Ways But One

People look at me and then they walk away
But if they think before they walk
They'd notice that we're the same
In all ways but one.

Emma Kyle (13)
Glenlola Collegiate School

The Gift

Daily he sits at his loom,
Same cracked leather seat,
His only companion a cat.

Furrowed brow and wrinkled cheek,
Still deft of hand and foot,
The threads he weaves are as silver as his hair.

Click, clack back and forth the noisy shuttle flies,
The silver yarn is woven
With greatest love and care.

Finished now and satisfied with the piece that he's created,
A wedding gown so beautiful,
For someone very special.

Sarah Blair (12)
Glenlola Collegiate School

Walk In My Shoes

Each and every day that passes
I cannot shake the sadness.
My friends have died
And so shall I
If my hunger doesn't go away.

But then I said that yesterday
There is nothing to keep me alive,
So how can I survive?

This morning I awoke,
I was so upset that this I spoke,
This world is not worth living in,
So let's just throw it in the bin.

Leah Kirkwood (13)
Glenlola Collegiate School

Walk In My Shoes!

Why don't you walk in my shoes,
The pain I see,
People living in poverty,
Babies dying days after birth,
Mothers and fathers on their last days.

Why don't you walk in my shoes,
No food to eat,
Children begging for money,
Fathers head out to work,
Where they get hardly any pay.

Why don't you walk in my shoes!
Disease spreading every day!
With no pay,
Each day a nightmare.

Melissa Keenan (14)
Glenlola Collegiate School

The Pennydrop Man

On the corner of Treetop Lane
The Pennydrop Man sits in the rain.
He is quite smart, but often labelled insane.
He sits there begging on Treetop Lane.

On the corner of Treetop Lane
The Pennydrop Man lies in pain.
His legs are broken; he is now lame.
He lies there sleeping on Treetop Lane.

On the corner of Treetop Lane
There was a funeral, but no one came.
He died alone, lacking fame
And he dies there peacefully on Treetop Lane.

Katherine McKnight (11)
Glenlola Collegiate School

Walk In My Shoes

Look at the streets,
What do you see?
People
Sitting all alone,
Sitting in despair
At the
Loss of the
Families.
Begging from the
Rich.
We are
Poor
So
Help us
Please
By sending
Food,
Money,
Love,
Care
To stop
This
Living nightmare!
Stop hunger
And weakness,
Disease and death
From trying to get
To
Us.
Help,
Help!

Jenny Gwynne (14)
Glenlola Collegiate School

Down By The Coast

Over mountains - through the trees,
Glimmering stones - shimmering seas,
Cotton wool clouds - candy coves,
Beautiful beach - down by the coast.

Gemma Wingar (14)
Glenlola Collegiate School

The Wilderness

Striking silhouette of a distant doorway
Amongst and afield with treacherous treason,
Skies so still but filled with fear,
Water is lacked, but it still grows on.

Immense anticipation crosses the land,
But still the birds sing a soft song,
So let it be far and wide that
Creatures sit side by side.

Emma Webster (14)
Glenlola Collegiate School

Meadow

In the distance - glistening waters,
Green pastures - golden reeds,
Swaying trees - caught in the breeze,
Hawk's home - ravens' roost.

Lauren Scott (14)
Glenlola Collegiate School

Bird On Branch

Bitter winter - huddled and warm,
Brown as bark - gold as corn,
Feather coat - belly to throat,
Eyes of glass - watch the grass,
Tiptoeing on thorns - balancing and delicate,
Breeze blasts - ready to fly at last.

Natassia Young (14)
Glenlola Collegiate School

Curious Crow

Feathers as black as death,
Beak as sharp as blades,
Staring out of focused eyes,
Claws with a texture like the branch it grips onto.

Holly Clark (14)
Glenlola Collegiate School

To The Top

Travelling high over - rocking ramps,
Reaching the sky - chilling clouds,
Breaking particles - falling furiously,
Near the edge - something silent,
River down below - rapidly roaming,
Almost there - continuous climbing.

Becky Smyth (14)
Glenlola Collegiate School

I Saw An Elf

In the woods I saw an elf,
I asked him his name.
He said he wouldn't tell me,
Unless I played his game.

I wondered should I follow him
And see just where he took me.
But something in my mind said no,
He seemed rather seedy.

His body wasn't very big,
His feet were really smelly.
His voice was like a cackle
And my legs were like jelly.

I ran as fast as I could go,
He was nearer than I thought.
My heart was beating loudly,
I thought I had been caught!

I shouted to him, 'Let's be friends.'
He was extremely happy.
He gave me a ginormous hug,
Then said his name was Grappy.

Tara Baird (12)
Glenlola Collegiate School

The Victim

Brain barrier - badly bruised,
Torn T-shirt - aggressive and abused,
Frowned forehead - silent sobs,
Shelters shattered - lying lonesome,
Chattering chants - painful pulse,
Rich red runny - drip, drop, drip,
Nobody hears nothing - tearful, terrified eyes,
Slowly swallowing - dark, dark falling.

Ashley Martin (14)
Glenlola Collegiate School

Dear Mum

You're the best mum in the world,
(In case you didn't know).
I am writing this poem
To make sure that my love shows.

You always make me happy
When I'm feeling sad.
You seem to calm me down
When I'm feeling mad.

When you go away
Maeve and I don't mind,
Because we always remember
You're the best one of your kind.

So when you're in America
Take this poem with you,
So you can comfort Dad
If he gets lonely too.

Laura-Jane Stacey (13)
Glenlola Collegiate School

The Linen Museum

Ghost-like linen on display,
Behind the glass tucked away.
Curse hung low, a scary spell,
Rumours whispered, here to tell.

A spinning wheel, we stood to stare,
Stories that stood up our hair.
Gaping painting no two the same,
Our memories from the Linen Museum.

Emily Allen (12)
Glenlola Collegiate School

The Killing Machine

Slowly, smoothly,
The killing machine glided past.
Long, grey body,
With bluish streaks due to the sun.
Underneath, all was a dreamy white.
The black, fathomless eye,
Watched my every movement.
Gills rippled,
Bloodless wounds in the steely skin.
Teeth sparkling,
Sharp enough to go through steel.
An angel of death,
With so many victims to its name.

Rachel Graham (17)
Glenlola Collegiate School

King Of The Sky

Resplendent in his palace,
The King of the Sky sits, as a crimson dawn breaks out.
Ready to make his exciting entrance,
His loyal subjects surround him,
Protecting, from the gaze of those below.
The shining crown rests upon his noble bow,
Filling the atmosphere with a heavenly glow.
The home of the gods makes a perfect throne room.
Night never falls in his kingdom,
The Earth seems but a tiny speck
Blurred on the rosy horizon.
As midnight colours bleed into a watery wash,
The sun crowned King of the Sky!

Sarah McVeigh (18)
Glenlola Collegiate School

Snowed In

A warm crackling fire blazed hungrily in the living room,
Soft snow fell in blankets whilst powerful winds
Whistled down our chimney breast.
The power was out all around.
A blanket of darkness fell on our little town
And only the silvery moonlight remained.
Terry teased me and shouted, 'Boo!'
I jumped like a small child.
Outside the roof tiles whizzed through the air
And smashed into a mosaic of tiny pieces.
Fearsome waves rolled in and crashed high
Above the harbour wall destroying all in their path.
More damage will occur for my town as Winter
Searches for more of her victims.

Alison McKibben (18)
Glenlola Collegiate School

Innocent Flower

Innocent flower,
Vaulting ambition,
Murder, evil and unnaturalness,
Humorous, drunken partner.

Tension and suspense for audience,
Innocent flower,
Macduff and Banquo in trouble,
Murder, evil and unnaturalness.

Thunder and lightning,
Tension and suspense for audience,
Lady Macbeth and Macbeth evil,
Macduff and Banquo in trouble.

Tory Hughes (16)
Glenlola Collegiate School

My House Is Haunted

My house is haunted,
Sweets get eaten,
Drinks are drunk
Not by us.

My house is haunted,
Floorboards creak,
Things move,
No one's there.

My house is haunted,
Shadows on the walls,
Noises at night
Coming for me.

My house is haunted
By two dead goldfish
Buried in the garden,
I killed them.

My house is haunted,
Tonight they'll come,
A scream in the night,
Then deathly silence.

Kathryn Hunter (13)
Glenlola Collegiate School

Walking In My Shoes

Here I am lying in the ground,
This is all I have found.
It's cold and lonely out here,
It makes me fear.

Just look around.

Sarah Macauley (14)
Glenlola Collegiate School

Footsteps

Footsteps, footsteps,
Where do they lead?
They could be an animal's
Or a person in need?

Footsteps, footsteps
Where do they go?
They could be a hunter's
Who is lying low.

Footsteps, footsteps
Whose are they
I'll find out
If it takes all day.

Footsteps, footsteps
They end just here.
Whosoever they are
They must be near.

Footsteps, footsteps
I've found whose they are,
They belong to a tiny
Budgerigar!

Rachel Atwell (13)
Glenlola Collegiate School

Threads Of Time

The skilled craftsmen are in control
Spinning the threads of time,
Weaving the story together,
Sewing together the pieces of life,
To complete, in the end, a tapestry,
A picture perfect.

Abi Ballantine (13)
Glenlola Collegiate School

Lightning

I'm sitting in a very dark cave
And I pray to the Lord that I can be brave
For the lightning strikes with all its might,
Large flashes of very bright light
Appear to me before my eyes
As the skies above me start to cry.

Nature's revenge is very strong,
Just the quality that I long,
As the lightning gets nearer
I quiver with fear,
I shout for guidance,
Silence.

But soon the lightning storm passes by,
All is well, no need to cry.
I venture out, the skies are clear,
So I start walking, home is near.
I arrive and greet my friends,
I made it through, right to the end.

Anna Harmon (17)
Glenlola Collegiate School

Stars

Sparkling like dots on a sea of black,
Colourful
Like a peacock's feathers.
I wonder
What it feels like
To be floating
On a bed of darkness
To be washed about
Like seaweed in a stormy sea,
To be
Bright as a light that shines on forever.

Megan McCreedy (13)
Glenlola Collegiate School

Love

Love is a glint in the corner of the eye,
Knowing someone's every movement, a silent sigh.
It's a feeling of passion beyond all control,
It captures the mind, the body, and even the soul.

Love has the power to send shivers to the spine,
It's nobody else's - this love is mine.
Love is identifying just by touch,
Knowing you really need someone all that much.

Love is powerful and so, so strong,
It never lets go, just clings on and on.
Love is held in the stars of the night,
Love is blind - a loss of sight.

Love is like a growing flower,
Gets stronger every second, ever minute, every hour.
Love is Romeo and Juliet longing to be together,
Now above with the angels together forever.

Ashley Thompson (17)
Glenlola Collegiate School

In The Broken Shadow

In the broken shadow
Muscles swell
Cleanline, shaped
Sleek, shining, bristling silver
Rock slide
Downhill shot.
Wonderful, whistle, swell
Lifted lurching, curl
Heavy horns, hill
Cropped cleanline
Great grizzlies
Jagged, bulging, bristling, bawling.

Tanya Baker (16)
Glenlola Collegiate School

Fear

At night in the dark
When there's a scuttle at your bed
Your body goes rigid,
Is it all in your head?

At someone's house
You shiver and you're sick
As you watch a scary movie
And your mind plays tricks.

When you're on a boat
In the middle of the lake
And the waves are crashing
Your body starts to shake.

Fear is an awful, horrible thing
It makes you have goosebumps and butterflies
But you may find
It's a whole lot of lies,
All made up in your mind.

Karina Magee (11)
Glenlola Collegiate School

Memories

Frayed around the edges,
Soft puff of bluish hair, set like was tradition
Beckoned me to sit with her
On one bony, frail knee.
The clothes she wore as old and soft and comforting
As she was to me.
The elbows were in holes,
That wool that died with her.
Now only a red, shiny memory in a jar remains
To remind me of that day.

Claire MacDuff (17)
Glenlola Collegiate School

D-Day 60th Anniversary - A Fight For Freedom

As they said their goodbyes with tearful eyes,
Holding their mother while she cries.
Showing such courage while facing their fears,
Fighting for the freedom, of their peers.

Together they stood fighting as one,
Friends, brothers, a father and son.
They did not run or show their white flags.
Their spirits kept high by each man's gags.

Death, heartache, fear and sorrow,
The torment of a new tomorrow.
Just some of the feelings our men had.
The fight for freedom driving them mad.

It's alright for us we'll never know,
Just how much courage those men had to show.
The freedom we'll have in the future and have had in the past,
Thanks to those men will forever last.

As a child of today in debt to each man who fought,
I'd like to thank them for a present that could not have been bought.
I now have the freedom that I could have been denied,
I salute the soldiers who are living and those who died.

Sian Brennan (13)
Glenlola Collegiate School

Forest And Sea

Through the wood - under the green
Billowing bushes - lovely scene
Shaking leaves - whistling wind
Glistening reflector - screaming silence.

Carmen Tang (14)
Glenlola Collegiate School

The Linen Museum

The spinning wheel spun like a merry-go-round,
Wool tied like a boat to the shore.
The weaving machines going clicky, clack,
Tapping coming from the door.

The stories were sharp
And made you shiver.
When someone tapped you on the back
It made you quiver.

We heard of the fighting,
The heads and the ghosts.
The Egyptian linen,
Stories told by our host.

We saw all the pictures
Pinned up on the wall,
It looked like they were following us
All the way down the hall.

We had a good day
And we learnt quite a lot.
We finished the day
Tying wool in a knot.

We made lovely bookmarks,
All colours and new.
We had a great day
So we all want to thank you.

Rebecca Bingham (13)
Glenlola Collegiate School

The Rise And Fall

The tide breaks - it hits the sandy shore
Torrent of salt - crashing on the soft, spiky bed
A mermaid's hand grabs it - pulls it out again
Leaving behind - all the treasures of the sea.

Lauren Scott (14)
Glenlola Collegiate School

A Thunderstorm

All alone in the middle of the forest, lost and afraid,
The wagoner quietly reassures his horse,
But it is he who needs reassurance.
He cannot help but notice the sky,
The dark clouds eating away the daylight
Till the entire sky is blanketed in thick, black menace.
He knows too well what will happen,
His horse won't like Mother Nature's dark side
And neither will he . . .
Suddenly, unexpectedly there is a flash,
A long streak of blue lightning illuminates the sky.
The terrified horse's nostrils flare wildly
As the lightning is reflected in the whites of its eyes.
The panicking wagoner tries to still the crazed horse,
But his attempts are wasted.
A long, loud clap of thunder is heard,
Rumbling fiercely, echoing through the sky,
An awesome, powerful, frightening sound.
The horse kicks in terror,
Now completely out of control.
The wagoner whispers a silent prayer,
To find their way out . . . alive.

Elizabeth Patterson (17)
Glenlola Collegiate School

My Dream

Hooves thundering - wind wailing
Grass swaying - hair matting
Laughing, smiling - looking free
Tall trees - lapping sea
Wandering round - on the ground
Prancing, bouncing - splashing waves.

Rachael Prentice (14)
Glenlola Collegiate School

The End Of The Day

Endless horizon - sunset silhouettes
Mist covered mountains - peaceful pastures
Yellow heaven - significant stillness
Solid ground - breathtakingly beautiful
Rippled sky - Heaven's high.

Alison Rea (14)
Glenlola Collegiate School

The Dress

The dress was so pretty
From oh so long ago.
She stared at it in wonder,
Where did her man go?

That hole inside her grew
As she put away her dress.
Will that day come again
And will it be the best?

Now the dress is on display
In a glass case.
Made of linen long ago,
Embroidered with long lace.

Gillian McBride (12)
Glenlola Collegiate School

Deep Under The Sea

Deathly pale - cloudy corals
Reflecting sun - summer sky
Stealthily swimming - pounding on prey
Marine blue - crashing through
Splish, splash - wish, wash
Listen to the sound - feel the tranquillity.

Jayne McKee (15)
Glenlola Collegiate School

Dreams . . .

With linen, so fine, white and delicate
Like a blanket weaved with clouds,
Like a horizon it shines bright,
Like a moon lighting up each night . . .

It is a worker's bible, each person longs to hold,
It's a great, giant statue, mind of precious gold . . .

Finest, divine and beautiful
Just like a diamond ring,
Just like the sweet, pure sound
Of a bird about to sing.

Pharaoh's linen, finest, the best
Like a necklace across a human chest.

The museum is not the one for fame,
But the myths and legends tell the story the same.

Abbi McCallum (12)
Glenlola Collegiate School

Nothing On Earth

I'm all alone,
Sad and poor,
I can see through my flesh
To my skinny bone.
I'm in despair,
Is there anyone out there?

My feelings have taken me away,
I feel I'm at death's door.
I'm being pulled away from life
Into a dark and gloomy room.

I have no food,
Nothing on Earth will do me any good.

Rebekah Heath (13)
Glenlola Collegiate School

Burnt Umber

Sandy dunes - slowly strolling
Blistering heat - burning orange
Set in the horizon - treading softly
Caramel coat rough and wiry - large feet sinking
Eyelashes blinking - warm and whistling
Gently blowing - breathing deeply.

Julie Scott (14)
Glenlola Collegiate School

Gold Linen

Spin it fast,
Spin it strong,
Spinners, weavers spinning all day long,
Beautiful maidens with flax-like hair
Spinning gold to mend a tear,
Cloth to make a wedding gown
Of pure linen, golden
The colour of a majesty's crown.

Claire Boardman (13)
Glenlola Collegiate School

Deadly Drought

Blinding beam - withered weeds
No healthy life - no living thing
Crowded cactus - burning bushes
Bony background - flaming atmosphere.

Claire Stannage (14)
Glenlola Collegiate School

Walk In My Shoes

Walk in my shoes,
I'll tell you what I see.

Distress, hunger, sickness,
Separation, dehydration,
That is what I see.

But there is so much
More pain and suffering,
So take a walk with me
And these will be a few things
Only that you see!

Rebekah Hammond (13)
Glenlola Collegiate School

Autumn

Conkers are lying on the ground,
Dead leaves are crisp and rustling,
Sycamore seeds parachute down,
Bonfires are blazing and crackling.

Hedgerow berries, soft and ripe,
Like gleaming jewels in the soft sunlight,
A patchwork quilt are the fields of gold,
Awaiting the farmer, their harvest foretold.

Earth's rich colours soon will fade,
Her morning mist's a heavy veil,
Days are shorter, so much colder,
The fruitful season is now over.

Sarah Brennan (17)
Glenlola Collegiate School

Desert Dies

Patchy puffs - darkened lights fade
Silhouettes show - tunnel of light glows
Slow marching - camels go
Raging roof - battles heat
As tired camels - struggle to meet
Loneliness calls - camels fall
Leaving land - standing tall.

Jannine Macfarlane (14)
Glenlola Collegiate School

The Rock Challenge

Shaking hands - deep breathing
Touch the tree tops - touch the clouds
Rough rocks - smooth hands
Secure harness - don't fall!
Death is feared - Heaven's near.

Rachel Pritchard (14)
Glenlola Collegiate School

Broken

Through the looking glass - shattered smile
Made up madness - hiding pain
Falling to pieces - broken-hearted strain
Going nowhere - lost, alone
Terrified tears - needing to go home
Shattered smile - pitiful pain
Looking once more - shameless shame.

Cassie Murphie (15)
Glenlola Collegiate School

Jewel Beetle

Grungy green - roasting red
Scary sight - wicked wings
Big black eyes - sleeked species
Buzzing beetle - with posture and pose
Carefully cruising - through the skies.

Loren McDowell (14)
Glenlola Collegiate School

Loneliness

Loneliness is a black hole in someone's heart,
The taste of a drop of cold blood,
A smell so sour like burning tyres.
The sight of a person crying
To their heart's desire.
A sound so empty that nothing can break it,
A touch of darkness like soft silk.

Nicole Mailey (12)
Glenlola Collegiate School

Linen

The spinning wheel is a roundabout going faster and faster
Driven on by the tireless spinner,
Working the magic of turning flax into yarn,
Yarn to become the finest linen,
Linen, ancient Egypt burial cloth,
Linen, supermodel choice.

Kerry Adrian (13)
Glenlola Collegiate School

Another Level

Along the crowded hall and down the stairs
To where
She knew that he would be.
She knew that he would be
Downstairs
Just sitting, as if he'd not a care
Or thought
For who was there
And who was not -
Just sitting.
And on his face he'd wear
That smile -
That smile that shared
With all downstairs
His lack of care
Or thought
(For who was there
And who was not.)
She knew that smile,
She knew his way -
His way
That never let him say,
'Come sit with me.'
She knew that he would never say,
'Come sit with me.'
Yet still along the hall and down the stairs
She went
Because she cared -
She cared about the boy downstairs.
She cared a lot -
Despite the fact he never seemed to give a thought
To who was there
And who was not . . .

Megan Gray (17)
Glenlola Collegiate School

A Linen Life

Round and round,
Round and round,
The spinning wheel goes,
In the day, in the night,
All of the fibres are being spun tight.

Over and under,
Over and under,
Weavers need to know,
This is how to weave the string,
This is why working hands sting.

Shine and shine,
Shine and shine,
This is what the sun should do,
To create snowy fields of linen
For all the men and the women.

Flax was life,
This was life,
Round, shine, over and under,
But how?
We only imagine it now.

Rebecca Lennie (12)
Glenlola Collegiate School

The Ghost Of The Linen Museum

Henry's the ghost of the linen museum,
You have to be alone in the hall to see him.
He's heard by people, his footsteps walking,
Raised voices of him and his friends talking.
But don't be alarmed, I've heard he's quite nice,
But be mean to him and he'll be gone in a trice!

Rebecca Blair (12)
Glenlola Collegiate School

Young Writers - Great Minds From Co Down

Egyptian Linen

It was made into linen by the wheel of a bike
And made into snow garments that the gods would like.
It was gold in the Egyptian times when King Tutt was in charge,
It was wrapped around pharaohs then they were put in their barge.

Anna Baird (12)
Glenlola Collegiate School

On Our Way

In the station you can't hear a thing,
Everyone is silent apart from a whisper,
The children are crying, the parents too.
We have but two cases the size of a bag
And around our necks there's a numbered tag.
We say our goodbyes and jump on the train
With a toot of the horn we're off on our way.
As we grow nearer we're all very sad,
But on the other hand we're glad.
We are escaping from the war
But we'll never see our family again.

Hannah Beattie (13)
Glenlola Collegiate School

You Cannot Walk

You cannot walk in my shoes
For I . . . I have no shoes.
I battled my way through World War I
And came home with no feet, no legs, no knees.
But I am thankful to someone like you,
Someone who listens, who gives, who cares.

Carly MacBratney (13)
Glenlola Collegiate School

Walk In My Shoes

When we see their hunger
We send them some food,
It probably never reaches them
But I really wish it could.

Holly Hunter (13)
Glenlola Collegiate School

Walk In My Shoes

Each day is like a film,
So much death and despair.
They say the same, I care
Yet they never really do.

Mum and Dad are gone,
So are Mark and John,
I won't be here for long.
Hunger is what took them
And it's coming back for me.

We'll be together in Heaven,
That is where we'll meet.
No hunger, pain, death, despair,
Happy as can be.

Lucy Kayes (13)
Glenlola Collegiate School

Walk In My Shoes I Say

Walk in my shoes I say
And see how bad my life is today,
Although I say today
This is my life, every day.

Monique Geddis (14)
Glenlola Collegiate School

Linen

You pull it and stack it,
You soak it and scutch it,
It makes such a racket,
You breathe the dust in.

You comb the white-grey hair
And spin it to thread,
You take special care,
In keeping it wet.

You weave it together
And a sheet comes off,
It's light as a feather,
You cut up the cloth.

Then bleaching and dyeing,
If you can afford it.
Then wait till it's drying
And sew it all up.

It's taken so long
And made such a mess,
But it's been worth it all
To make a linen dress.

Deborah Kinghan (13)
Glenlola Collegiate School

Flaming Fight

Through the square - heat bellows
Crackle, crunch - red ribbons flow
Glowing on your body - beams throughout the room
From your thinking machine - tingles to your toes.

Hannah Steenson (15)
Glenlola Collegiate School

Alone

Walk in my shoes,
I sit in the dark,
I'm all alone.
My parents are dead,
I'm all alone.
I live on the street,
I'm all alone.
No one's there,
I'm all alone.

Ruth Hooks (14)
Glenlola Collegiate School

A Mighty Mountain

Over misty mountains - and boggy heath
Billowing bunches - of brown trodden blankets
An ocean of wonder - winding roads
Sea of green grass - gentle and calm.

Etta Stevenson (15)
Glenlola Collegiate School

Haiku Chain

I despise writing
Poetry, it makes me sound
All so self-absorbed.

The buzzing machines
Sound like little men trying
Not to scream aloud.

My teeth feel as if
A small bird has flown in and
Raised its tiny chicks.

Heather Penn (16)
Glenlola Collegiate School

Young Writers - Great Minds From Co Down

Deep In The Mountains

Deep in the mountains
In the broken shadows,
Round the peak that looked so smooth
You hear the silent riding.

Up the river
Three miles away,
You climbed around
To find a clear space,
Afraid to look down,
Looking carefully at every yard.

Nicola Durieux (17)
Glenlola Collegiate School

Work

Work . . .
Was fun one day . . . a long time ago.
Now boring.
Always loved to go to work.
Though I have to make my own fun -
Wanted work
Friends thought would be fun.
But little did I know it would be
Hell.
The sky so grey.
Greyer than I have ever seen -
Every time I got angry I heard thunder and lightning
Everything my sister says to do I have to do.
Not so bad now.
Bit like school.
Like some of the teachers.
Wee bit like my wee sister -
I think it is just her age . . . I think.
I do enjoy work and school.
But not so much my wee sister.

Juneve Clark (14)
Kilkeel High School

Sectarianism Sucks!

Red, white and blue . . . green, white and gold
Will this diversity ever grow old?
To defend your religion you'll murder and fight
If you were truly religious, you'd know that's not right.
Shunning, stereotyping, bullying and more,
Guns, violence, bloodshed and gore.
Flags, flown high to annoy, intimidate,
You've seen it before, you can relate!
Division of the nation, cause: discrimination
Whatever happened to society's integration?
Your bigotry is wearing my patience thin,
How can you have so much hatred within?
Or is this all an act to impress your friends?
Then it's clear to fit in you'll go to all ends.
But if you agree with all I've just said,
Stand up for what you believe in, instead.

Rebecca Cassidy (16)
Kilkeel High School

A Modern Fool's Riddle: King Lear

(In response to the fool's advice to lear in 'King Lear': a modern equivalent)

Be modest about your belongings,
Do not throw away everything you own,
Walk more,
Leave the car at home,
Listen to others' opinions - even if you don't believe it!
Know what to say -
Know when to stop talking.
Gamble moderately,
Leave drink, drugs and desire -
Stay indoors
- You will gain more,
Than you could ever expect.

Emma Jane McCavery (16)
Kilkeel High School

When Death Comes . . .

Short breaths,
eyes fixed,
it's crawling inside,
eating away,
limiting time
destroying days.

Time is short,
life is full,
grab each moment,
don't let it go.

Appreciate each person
otherwise they'll never know
how grateful you were
before you had to go.

Louise Orr (15)
Kilkeel High School

Tick

Silently I wait in wonder,
Not knowing when it will be.
But suddenly right in front of me,
The clock hand moves with a gracious tick.
Like a flower beginning to open,
Or the rising of the morning sun.
A sudden prick from a long, sharp pin,
The loud crack from a bite of some candy.
That moment I realised that time ticks by,
Not caring what happens to me.

Alison McConnell (16)
Kilkeel High School

Death

Death and disappointment hung over my heart like a veil,
As I stood covered in a cloak of darkness pierced with stars,
The friendly feline faded away,
Into a maze of dreams, memories and ambitions,
Never to be seen again!

The cold thud of the damp earth,
As it's pulled from its hellish domain,
Echoed around in the stillness of the night.
A thousand needles pricked my skin,
As the wind whispered gently across my face.

That night I realised life is precious,
And a gift from above,
Appreciate it well,
Because it can be gone in a flash.

Linda Clements (15)
Kilkeel High School

A School Trip To Killowen

We went to Killowen on a school bus,
Which was full with bags
and other stuff.
I shared a room with Rachel, Megan
and Holly,
We had a good laugh and were saying things
like 'Oh golly!'
The first thing we did was go to our dorm,
a few hours later it looked like a storm.
We went bouldering in the Bloody Bridge,
After a while we were floundering.
Killowen was cool, even though
it was a bit like school.

Hollie Donaldson (11)
Kilkeel High School

ILL

Hot, restless, miserable.
Can't eat or sleep.
Impatiently willing freedom from torture.
Endurance frustrates.
Home alone;
Tossing and turning;
Begging time to fly.
Hearing distanced,
All murmurs and drones.
Mocking repetition 'tick, tock'.
Dragging your weak body to the
Cool, smooth haven of your bathroom floor.
Waiting, waiting.
Nausea and stale aftertaste.
Back to bed:
Hot, restless, miserable.
Ill, we realise how fragile we are.

Grace Hanna (16)
Kilkeel High School

Gardening

I saw Dad trim the hedge.
I thought it looked simple.
I soon found out it was not.
The work was easy, but the hedge-trimmer was heavy.

I saw Johnny cutting the grass, that I had just cut.
I thought to myself, *what is he doing?*
Then I realised he was just finishing it off.

Then I realised that I should not say anything
About something until I have tried it myself.
Because you may change your mind.

Don't make fun of the work other people do,
Until you have tried it yourself.

Gareth Allen (15)
Kilkeel High School

In A Beautiful World

Radiant stares of delicate, treasure-bronze eyes
Capture a star's glisten as it lingers in the sky
His soul silently levitating in the vastness of the night
In a beautiful world, as moonlight becomes him.

Slender, sunbeam satin strands, lightly dust his skin
His beauty, a fascinating portrait, from hairline to chin
A chameleon of elegance; a carved stone heart within
In a beautiful world, as moonlight becomes him.

Delicate passion flower petals fall with persistence
Sea of dreams in jasmine flowers, on wings of dove's eternal peace
Let down the shrouds of pretence; let the rays of truth come in
In a beautiful world, as moonlight becomes him.

The chilled winds lightly blowing, the night skies showering comets
Igniting a fiery blaze housed deep within the halls of his chest
Expanding the night's blackened walls, becoming darkness'
                                            sweet caress.
In a beautiful world, as moonlight becomes him.

Rain refreshes the shadows making the points of the leaves glitter
Earth perfumes itself afresh, as the night becomes dimmer
Gracefully watching every droplet on his damp skin shimmer
In a beautiful world, as moonlight becomes him.

Emeralds flow through the rivers of azure; transparent reflections strike
A mirage of perfect perfection, hovers distantly in the night
Highlighted by the Earth's glow and the darkness' ray of light.
In a beautiful world, as moonlight becomes him.

Donna Thompson (16)
Kilkeel High School

Ice Cream!

Ice cream is my favourite food,
Although it is not very good.
All of the facts I have unmasked,
'Bout how it puts on weight so fast.
And if I try to keep quite trim,
The future always looks so dim
With all these diets, you're all worn out,
But the mums say, 'You've nothing to complain about!'
If only they could understand,
To see my friends shove it down so fast,
It really is just torture for me,
So I ask you to listen to my plea.
Let me have some ice cream,
Ooh delicious ice cream!
I can feel the flavours on my tongue,
Tingling, jumping on the run.
But in a way they all are right,
I'll really give myself a fright,
If some morning I wake up
And end up looking like the ice cream tub
Next thing I'll be craving for the chocolate sauce!
Mauds, Morelli's, they all sound good.
Thinking of them puts me in a good mood
I'd better end this poem now,
I hear the ice cream calling
Come, come, now!

Louise Campbell (13)
Kilkeel High School

Chips

C runchy and tasty,
H ow delicious!
I think they're so yummy,
P inch of salt,
S crummy in your tummy!

Chloe McCullough (11)
Kilkeel High School

My School Trip

This is a poem
About Killowen
Leaving school
Am I a fool?
Get on the bus
Oh what a fuss
Arrived there
And fixed my hair
Oh the food
It was good
Watched a tape
Went to bed late
I fell out of bed
And thought I was dead
At the climbing Mrs Fry
Nearly did die
The rope traverse
Was fun in reverse
Going home
Not alone
Back to school
Oh no!

David Hanna (11)
Kilkeel High School

Cool Killowen

The class is going to Killowen
A bit boring, it beats English and
Art 'cause we have to learn sewing
When we got there it looked cool
A giant garden to play in
If I hadn't gone I would have been a fool
When time went by we were going canoeing
I was lucky I got to because
When he talked about work we started booing!

Christopher Cousins (11)
Kilkeel High School

Young Writers - Great Minds From Co Down

Petals Of Life

A world so imperfect, so bitterly split,
Torn totally apart by never-ending hate.
Words left unspoken, hearts remain broken,
As people reclaim their fate.

They think they are right,
They are seeing no wrong,
Why can't they understand?
While claiming power, they destroy the flower.
The sweet, budding flower of life.

Respect is required, respect is needed,
In order to restore the light.
The light of love wavers in everyone's heart
Seize it and cherish it - don't let it part.

If learned in youth, the love for others,
The future can be bright
And life can be lived with love and joy
And we can reclaim our might.

Generations are growing as time passes by,
But we can be the first to change.
Have the power, the feeling, the enjoyment of believing,
That we replenished the sweet, budding flower.

Stephanie McDowell (16)
Kilkeel High School

Pizza

P leased to eat it,
I ncredible taste,
Z ings in your mouth,
Z apping your taste buds
A way in seconds.

James Irvine (11)
Kilkeel High School

Him

The door crashed open
It was him
I had heard stories about his antics,
But had never seen him until now.
In he stormed, he was a hugely, intimidating man,
He was tall, thin with long matt-black hair.
His skin was mottled,
His nose was as long as a dog's
And his ears stuck out like the handles of a cup.
There was an evil glint in his eyes
And he wore a sadistic smile upon his face.
As he marched down the hall vigorously
He knocked down everything in front of him
Like a bull in a china shop.
The crowd scattered
As they were terrified at what might happen
If they stood in his way.
He marched beyond me
And picked a big man up like a pin.
Then threw him out the back entrance
He followed,
The door then smashed shut.
The crowd returned to normal.
But I was still shell-shocked at what had just happened,
And was still asking myself
Who was he?
What was he doing?
And how come the crowd paid no attention afterwards?

Daryl Parke (16)
Kilkeel High School

Heartache

The cold feeling of her wrinkly palms engaged my hand
As we drifted through the cold night air
Here we were a bond never to be broken
But now what's left of us, except a few memories here and there?

Where had all the time we spent together gone,
The laughs we shared and the tears we cried?
Everything was a blank to me, I was scared.
Why did she have to go?

The fresh smell of her new home enchants me
And I know some day I'll see her again
We'll talk and laugh about the time we've spent apart
And she'll always be looking over me.

I can hear her voice telling me to be strong
I know we'll meet again some day
But I had lost the most valuable part of my life
How could I go on? I needed her back.

Nadine Hewitt (16)
Kilkeel High School

Lasagne

Cheesy and delicious
That's how it smells!
Lovely and tomatoey,
Who can I tell?

Soft and runny,
That's how it feels!
Squidgy and watery,
Down to your heels.

Orange and red,
That's how it looks!
A book and a brick,
Now are you hooked?

Joshua Haugh (11)
Kilkeel High School

Darkness

The deep, black colour scares the happiness from me
Darkness thrusts the joyful moments away from me
Jealousy climbs up and releases a fierce beast
An animal so strong and powerful, no one has seen before.

Loneliness makes me hysterical
I try to grasp those brightened days
But the grim days enter my mind
Before me they bare their terrifying faces.

My fantasies and dreams are overcast by
Deep dark secrets, like bulky burdens.
Weighing me down so I can't move, then
Revenge grows on me.

It makes me the person I hate
Others are ungrateful, they have bright memories
Not like me
I have nothing, nothing at all.

Kerri Nicholson (11)
Kilkeel High School

My First Day!

First year!
Oh what a day,
As I walked to our allocated area
There were people running like wild animals.
As I sat there looking at my peers,
The bell rang.
A shot of fear ran through my body,
The beast my sister told me about was out,
It was hideous
It went about biting and snarling at people,
But luckily I didn't get bitten
And the monster passed me with just a snort.

Mark Cromie (14)
Kilkeel High School

Where?

She was always supposed to be there
Never left my side
We were joined at the hip
Very cute
Fat, but huggable
Fluffy
She put the apple in my pie
She loved drinking
Running the roads
And snoring on the sofa
But now she's gone
Why?
Lost? Where?
Or worse, dead!
Nine years now
Still no sign
My fault?

Sarah Jane Conn (14)
Kilkeel High School

Tiger

I am
Fighting machine
Antelope killer
Creator of blood
I harm everyone
I know
Screaming and banging sounds
From the prey as they hit the ground.
I kill at night and day
The angry tiger song
I harm everyone.

Chris Charleton (12)
Kilkeel High School

Filled With The Spirit - The Road To Revival

I speak not to my glory but to God's
For it is His promises that are fulfilled.
Only His name deserves to be honoured
For He is faithful, He will never lie.
'Lord, my hope is in You and You alone!'

We were gathered in an upper chamber
Singing, 'Let the Pentecostal fire fall'
When the Spirit came in wonderful power
And glorified Christ by filling this vessel
With power from on high; the Holy Spirit!

Like great surges of electricity,
Liquid love flowing through the entire body.
The Spirit who indwelt my conversion
Now gave power just as the prophets had said.
God's faithful, unchanging, sure and steadfast!

Getting back to the days of Pentecost,
A revival is heading to Ulster!
An army of ordinary people
Is assembling and their captain is Christ.

See the great clouds beyond the horizon,
Waiting to bring us the showers of blessing.
Satan trembles, he knows it is coming
But cannot stop God's omnipotent hand.

Believers, warriors in prayer, cry out:
'In the name of Jesus we have victory,
In the name of Jesus the demons flee
And soon the people of Ulster will see,
Jesus Christ, the son of God, it is He!'

We may lose our lives for the cause of Christ,
But in submission we say, 'Lord have thine own way!'

Andrew Clements (17)
Kilkeel High School

Holiday

Butterflies start to flutter,
While the heavens cry outside.
But we don't worry,
Soon we will see
The fire in the sky.

Engines roar; excitement grows.
Ears pop.
The plane leaves the ground.
Our dark world is left behind,
While the hours on the giant bird
Seem to fly by.

We have arrived
It's a completely different world.
Skin gets burnt off us.
Everything's so strange,
In this new world.
We ran away to this,
But what for?

Diane McMurray (14)
Kilkeel High School

The Flapping Fish!

What is a flapping fish?
Its head, quite small with bloodshot eyes
It fins, sharp as a knife whizzing through water
Its body is like a long sharp saw
Its mouth, so small you can barely see it
Its teeth, like the bristles of a small comb
Its dorsal fin, splashing above the water.
It soars through the water like a bat flapping its wings
It approaches the tiny fish like a flash of lightning.
Its tail flaps above the water as it sinks to the bottom to find its food!

Joanna Reilly (12)
Kilkeel High School

Shark

Grey and white hunter
Cruising through the oceans
Striking fear into any soul
It sees its prey

Shoots through the water
Like a speeding bullet
Splitting the waves
Menacing fin on the surface

Streamlined predator
Serrated teeth
Cut meat like a chainsaw
Man-eating monster

Catches a seal
Water instantly red
Feeding frenzy
Over in minutes.

Neil Newell (12)
Kilkeel High School

I Was Scared!

Thought more,
Wasn't looking forward to it.
New friends,
Have fun.
Was scared!
Everyone would laugh,
Make fun of me,
Hit me.

Got there.
Changed my mind!
My first day . . .
In a new school!

Danielle Rogers (14)
Kilkeel High School

The Poison Poem

The repugnant invasion
Thick green gunge
Oozes from the forbidden fruit.

Drawn in,
Lured.
I had to take a bite.

Fooled by its enticing glow,
Its burning poison corroded my tongue,
My teeth fizzed as they dissolved.
Its tongue-curdling taste trickled down my throat.
Toxicity began to pump through my blood
Like a ravaging bull.

Choked by its grasp,
Commanded by its power.
It now controlled my fate.

The desperate murmur of my heartbeat,
As its hungry mouth devoured my flesh
Searing pain conquered my body.

Poison's tempting evil . . .
Victorious.

Rachel Nicholls (15)
Kilkeel High School

Elephant

What is an elephant?
Its head, a giant boulder,
Its neck, a gigantic crane,
Its tusks are hooks,
Its skin is rough and lined,
Its run is a thundering earthquake,
Its trunk is a long tube that makes the noise of a foghorn.

Ryan Cunningham (13)
Kilkeel High School

Twenty Pieces Of Silver

I am watching you,
Every day I look out for you,
But you are too busy to see.
I spend my time following you
Every hour of my life is devoted to you,
But you ignore me.

I sit behind you
In that empty seat in class,
I whisper the answer in your ear,
I cry for your soul,
My own dear Son's body broken
So that you could snigger and jeer.

When you feel that shiver up your spine,
Hair rising on the back of your neck,
It's just me reminding you
He was bought for twenty pieces of silver,
Does mankind recollect?

Emma Campbell (16)
Kilkeel High School

The Dog I Used To Want!

I've always dreamt of having a dog
To play with on the beach.
It would have to be a boxer pup
Named Ruby.
My brother put me off my dream
When he got a Westie.
He has to:
Walk him,
Feed him,
Clean him
And brush him.
I don't want to do this
As I am lazy!

Lauren Shields (13)
Kilkeel High School

Young Writers - Great Minds From Co Down

That's When It Happened . . .

I used to love horses,
Until the day . . .
I fell off!
My stirrup came loose,
I panicked
My foot slipped out
'Slow, Chancer, slow!'
My heart started racing faster and faster
But he did too!
I was so scared!
I started to tremble
He was determined;
To get to the front
To beat the rest
To win!
Suddenly
That's when it happened . . .
I fell off!

Katherine Beck (13)
Kilkeel High School

New Girl

New girl
Everyone stared!
Was she from outer space
Without the funny green face?
She was slipping into thin air.
I didn't want to sit beside her.
But . . . first words she spoke
And the first smile she gave
. . . then I knew,
She wasn't an alien.
It was as if I'd known her for years.
My friend Anna.

Roberta Graham (15)
Kilkeel High School

The Swimming Dog

I was walking
My dad,
My dog,
Mourne Park.
Young . . .
Adventurous . . .
Smelling new smells . . .
Hearing new sounds . . .
The dog?
Couldn't swim.
Splash!
Fish in the river
All dogs
Could swim
She could swim!

John Graham (13)
Kilkeel High School

Fire

Innocent and harmless, 'nothing to worry about'
Transforms into something horrible and frightening.
What can I do to stop it?
Out of control, no way out, *help!*
The guilt was welling up inside me ready to explode
Smoke was rising higher by the second
Flames consuming everything in sight
I was going mental, panicking
What was going to happen?
Everyone's life in my hands,
But it was 'only a bit of fun'
I just stood there staring at them, not saying a word.
They appeared from the flashing lights; it was over.
I started running, running, never to look back.
They saved everything; it was their job and their destiny.
That's when I promised never to light fires again.

Andrew Smyth (14)
Kilkeel High School

Death

A dark, gloomy house,
I was only young.
Had never dealt with a death
I couldn't believe she died.
She was my granny.
Dark clouds covered the house,
I couldn't get a breath.
My mother took me to see her,
In the coffin.
I was afraid!
The last time I was going to see her?
Tears filled my eyes,
'Goodbye,' I cried.
From that day on I realised
We all are going to die.
We can't live forever.
Get on with life;
Deal with problems!

Ruth White (13)
Kilkeel High School

Hunger

Something we all get,
When you feel it you must feed it.
But not to make it grow,
To shrink the pain,
But you have to be careful,
Don't overfeed the monster
Or it will grow as big as you can imagine.
So just remember, when you're hungry
Don't let the monster tell you to eat.
You ignore its angry voice
So you can be happy.

Kathryn Jess (11)
Kilkeel High School

My Boat Trip

It was a miserable day
Just like any other day,
But this day was special.

I was sweltering to death on a bus
Waiting to enter
The dreadful mouth of the
Stena Line.

I was really excited
At the same time worried
It was a big boat
I was a small kid.

When I was aboard
It wasn't that bad.
I could hear people chatting.
I could smell the delicious smell of
Burger King
I could almost taste it in my mouth.

Didn't want to walk around the ship
I was too tired
I was too bored.
Was I going to make it to England?
Of course I would.

Daniel Ogle (14)
Kilkeel High School

Candy

C andy comes in all different shapes and flavours
A nd tastes delicious in my tummy and everyone eats it.
N aughty boy, you stole from the sweet jar.
D ad, brother Luke is turning purple
Y ou'd better call 999.

Alex Russell (12)
Kilkeel High School

Young Writers - Great Minds From Co Down

Christmas Eve Slips Slowly By

Snow is falling heavily down,
Joyful children running around,
Shouting, cheering, voices galore,
As Christmas Eve slips slowly by.

Movements vary - none are the same,
The little ones play many games,
While parents pretend to be calm
And Christmas Eve slips slowly by.

Mixed tastes spread round the cosy room -
There's turkey, puddings and the pie,
But best of all the children shout
That 'Christmas Eve is slipping by.'

Excitement and much happiness
All muddled up in one,
Fill all our hearts as Christmas Day
Dawns bright and clear at last.

Laura Shannon (15)
Kilkeel High School

Excited

I am very excited, it's my trip away,
It's with the school, for more than a day.

Everyone's happy, making lots of noise,
Especially with those strange little boys.

All those games waiting to be played,
It is worth all the money we paid.

Soon I will be back home in bed,
Then there is nothing more to be said.

Laura Herron (11)
Kilkeel High School

The Bat

Hanging by its feet, its sleeps like a horse all day,
Awakens at dusk, then searches all night,
Like a mouse it scrambles for food.
With wings of skin,
The hunter's blind night begins.

For this unseeing predator, sound leads the way.
Food is found with a high-pitched voice.
This small but scary creature strikes fear in all,
Its mythical background of blood sucking is spooky
But not in this country, no sucking at all.

So feel sorry or scared of our blind friend
And hope he flies safely home,
To a dark damp cave that is his home to rest,
But remember,
Its ears not eyes see the best.

David Glenny (13)
Kilkeel High School

Red

Red is the velvet rose
Fragrancing the air.
Red are the shining apples
Growing abundantly on the tree.
Red sparks the glow of the winter's fire
Touching others with its warmth.
Red gushed the blood from wounds
Of those who are hurt.
Like anger brewing in an eye,
Its beauty lights up the night sky.
Bitter tasting yet full of richness
Red rages yet showers rays of love.

Laura Hanna (16)
Kilkeel High School

The Dieter

There it was,
Waiting for me in the shop window,
I could almost hear it whispering, 'Eat me, you know you want to.'
I stood there staring at it.
My mouth watered, mmm . . . chow mein.

I can imagine the soft, succulent noodles in my mouth,
The juice squirting out of the chicken
And the bean sprouts when I bite them.
The crunchy onions,
Mmm . . . onions,
I love onions.

I can't, I have to, I must,
Give it to me,
I can't, I won't,
I have to get it,
Give it to me.

The mouth-watering goodness
A mixture of tenderness, crunchiness and soft noodles,
The wait is over.
Now I had it, my precious,
It was great.

Ryan McAtee (13)
Kilkeel High School

Night-Time Poem

The night was like thin ice,
The branches banging against the windows,
The screech of someone in pain,
The car horn is a sign of dark danger,
The wind was like a fan,
Destroying the heat inside the house.

Philip Main (13)
Kilkeel High School

The Dieter

I close my eyes as I pass
The ice cream parlour.
It was no use,
My eyes were magnetised to the window.
There it stood in all its elegance
A mound of colour,
A rainbow on a plate.
The chocolate-smothered strawberries
Lay embedded in the snow,
Awaiting to be rescued.
My eyes followed the syrup,
Which oozed its way over the surface
Like a fire spreading in hay.
My instinct took over my willpower
And lured me into the shop.
The bell which rang when the door opened
Also rang in my head,
Informing me to go for it.
Waiting to fulfil my mouth's desires
I bit my lip in anticipation.
I sat motionless,
Savouring every flavour and texture.
The crumbly chocolate melted
Making the combination complete.
'I wasn't a dieter,
How easy it was to fall back in temptation.'
Guilt overwhelmed me
Like the pride of a lion.
The once luxurious flood of flavour
Disappeared to a sour taste - bitterness!
After all a leopard can't change its spots.

Leanne McConnell (14)
Kilkeel High School

The Burnhouse

A second in time slips by
A life is lost.
In previous moments that animal lived
Like a carefree butterfly
But now . . .
Lifeless

The final journey has begun
The bare road looms ahead
Like a silent, empty future
The rain pounds on the windscreen
As though the heavens are shedding tears.
The destination creeps closer
Like a tiger waiting to snare its prey.
Finally it overwhelms
Huge grey stone buildings;
Ice-cold surroundings.

Dozens of dead carcasses are strewn along the ground
A terrible stench fills the air
So horrible it washes over your taste buds
Causing you to retch in disgust
The trailer shudders as the body is removed
The forklift drags his limp head along the ground
Like a rag doll being held by a child
The remains are dragged from view
Preventing us from witnessing haunting images
Of the raging, red-hot fire
Burning innocent lives

That day I went to the Burnhouse.

Laura Beck (15)
Kilkeel High School

Innocence

It looked so innocent,
like a four-year-old toddler playing with paint.
Wasn't I wrong!
The remote taste was . . .
. . . tongue-curdling,
like cream that had been left for weeks and gone off.
Revolting!
As the thick, lumpy substance . . .
. . . moved through my body,
the roaring was overwhelming!
The roaring rage, was like a lion out hunting its prey.
It churned round my stomach,
making me feel diseased.
Devouring the inside of my stomach away.
It scalded me . . .
. . . as though I had just walked over burning ashes
in my bare feet.
Feeling like toxic waste trickling . . .
. . . down my throat, choking me.
All I could see was death looking . . .
. . . closer
. . . and closer,
staring me in the face.
My stomach screamed in terror as the venom was
destroying my body.
I had never felt so rotten!
I never knew such an innocent food could
cause so much terror.
Innocent, but deadly!

Claire Annett (14)
Kilkeel High School

A Ladle Full Of Medicine

Dagger slicing through my flesh,
Leaving his own mark so deep,
Scarring with his deadly rust,
Oozing vomit from my side.

Ploughing through my inmost parts,
Tearing, ripping . . . churning blood,
Gnawing through my belly wall,
While I fight me to defend.

Greedy - with his hungry jaws
Biting s-s-slowly
Through my nerves.
Leaving just his deadly ache
Surging through my body frail.

Worse this hypocritical cure,
Than his reason for attack.
Long now he has his revenge,
On the ailment which I had.

Ruth Shannon (14)
Kilkeel High School

The Moonlight

I see a silver moon
Which shimmers on the sea
It is enclosed with sparkling diamond jewels.
The sea has a furious, foaming temper
Its temper thumps against the harbour walls
The ships sway side to side.
Suddenly it's all quiet
The silver moon shines
High for a little while longer.

Andrew Greene (13)
Kilkeel High School

Guardian Angels From Above

Everybody has one person in life,
Who pushes them all the way.
Who helps them be the best that they are,
And will fight with them each day.
You know that without that person in your life,
You could easily drift away
And give up hope for the future
And wouldn't care about today.

But whenever you see this special person:
The wonders and beauties of life shine through
And you never want to be parted from them,
Because they mean everything to you.
They lift away the burdens of life
And when they leave, your heart will ache.
But this is a price which must be paid,
For being a gift like them so precious in life.

Rebecca McKee (15)
Kilkeel High School

Sleep

My fleecy pyjamas soft against my skin.
The smell of freshly washed sheets.
All I can see is darkness.
All I can hear is silence.
Mind working overtime.
Soon worries forgotten.
Brain switches off for the day.
Worries fade away.
I float off to my paradise of dreams.

Claire Quinn (15)
Kilkeel High School

Worth It

The long awaited brings tension,
Sweaty palms and deep breaths.
Preparing so fast to bring it nearer,
Too impatient to wait, but yet it's too soon.
Time slips through those sweaty fingers,
Adrenaline rushes through my veins.
I let my whole body bubble with irritated excitement.

But all of a sudden those bubbles are burst.
Standing in the sidelines, it's too close for comfort.
I want to turn back, I can't cope!
I need more time, I'm not ready!
But there's no way back, I can't escape.
The crowd who crave more are silenced
By the echo of my throbbing pulse.
They are all out there. Waiting.
My body freezes, my chest tightens,
I can't respond, I can't breathe.
Until a trickle of sweat slices my neck,
Pinching me back into reality.
Stepping out of the dark, clammy air of confusion
And into the bright fresh feel-free atmosphere
I let the spotlight blind all nerves
And noise of music scare all fears.
I let go, forget who I am,
And I flourish.
It was worth it.

Emma Annett (17)
Kilkeel High School

Sparkling Fireworks

Sparkling fireworks crackle in the sky
Animals fret from pops and bangs
Multicoloured sparks shooting by
Children crowded to play, on this happy
Hallowe'en night.

Philip Gordon (13)
Kilkeel High School

Fear

Lost in ecstasy, gazing high
Living shadows, stars so bright
Sounds so precious, breach my ear
As I listen, wait in fear.
Something's following, something black
Something breaking the dark of night.
Feeling its presence, I turn around
My cold, hard breath hitting damp, wet ground
Arms are numb; legs feel sore
Terror hits my very core.
Nerves are shattered, fear sets in
Emotion's gone, black will win,
But no, just wait . . .
Light returns
I watch and see a fire burn.
A secret blessing in disguise
Here to return my darkened eyes
The black is gone and feeling's back
It was only a cat walking over a crack.
The fire was really no more than a torch
Shining brightly from my own front porch,
I'm home again from my night-time walk
Turning the key in my front door's lock.

Steven Moorehead (14)
Kilkeel High School

My Bass

I love plugging the lead into my bass,
When I switch it on
I enjoy hearing the thrashing sound from the amp.
When I switch it on,
I like hearing the deep sound
When I play it.

Jordan McConnell (15)
Kilkeel High School

Giving In

It lay there
in a pool of cream
waiting to be rescued.
I walked into the shop,
its luscious smell filled
my nostrils.
My eyes closed.
I could feel the
strawberries melting in my mind.
My taste buds jumped in excitement.
No! I couldn't . . .
I have been doing so well.
I moved closer,
I heard the money jingling in my bag
as if it said, 'Do it, do it.'
Just then I felt a cold hand on my shoulder.
I jumped as fast as a cheetah,
It was my best friend.
She sat me down and ordered,
chatting away non-stop.
The food came, she told me to tuck in,
my diet it was ruined,
I felt so ashamed.

Jan McMurray (13)
Kilkeel High School

Night

The stars are like candles
On a winter's night.

The moon is like a clock face
Hanging on your bedroom wall.

The night sky is like a black sheet
With shadows and sounds all of
The night.

Gary Bingham (13)
Kilkeel High School

My Mind

Piercing through the land
infuriating!
Cars, houses, broken up like
a pile of rubble.
No one can stop it,
the child's screaming.
A flash of lightning
cold blood oozing out.
Quiet.
A sweet noise is
wavering!
'Who's there?' they scream.
'Kill them!'
Rain pitter-patters
the body floats
Away!
No one can help me
I'm lost!

Stephanie Annett (16)
Kilkeel High School

Night Poetry

The night was darker than
ever before tonight,
The light was lapping over
the sea,
The owls were hooting,
You could see the stars
shining.

You could hear the wolves
howling
It was like a robber's yelp
As he fell off the
roof.

Rodney Watterson (13)
Kilkeel High School

Young Writers - Great Minds From Co Down

The Owls Hooting

At night I stare out my window
I see a cat sitting on my wall.
The owls hooting
Cats miaowing
Dogs barking at every noise heard.
Cars racing
The TV blaring,
Echoing the sounds of a man at a rock concert.

The moon is shimmering,
A silver pebble all alone on an empty beach.
The owls hooting
Dogs barking
Cats miaowing
Cars racing
Outside my window.

April Bridges (13)
Kilkeel High School

The Moon, The Stars And The Dark Night

The stars are out
The sun has gone
The moon comes out from behind the cloud
Night is here, day has gone.

The stars are beaming
Like the sun glimmering
On the army's shields,
About to win the battle with the sun.
Everything is silent
Yes! They've won!

Night is here, the stars are bright
The owl comes out to hunt
The fox streaks through the meadow
Searching for something to eat.

Jason Tremlett (13)
Kilkeel High School

The Dieter

I walk by a cafe,
What do I see . . .
A tower of knickerbocker glory
I want it so bad, it's so tempting.
I must have the luscious tower of ice cream and fruits.
Decorated with . . . jewels.
The sticky syrup, sparkling like gold.

I stand there, my mouth watering . . .
I can taste the ice cream.
Stop it! Turn away.
I can't, it's too tempting.
The sparkler on top,
Crackling and sparking,
Like a firework.

I don't take my eyes off it.
I order it.
It's brought over . . .
My heart misses a beat.
My head says, 'Yes,'
My heart and stomach says, 'No.'

I scoop some ice cream and put it on my tongue.
It melts and I can taste the fabulous flavour.
As I chew, the fruits burst with flavour.
The fruits, cream and chocolate sauce scream out,
Eat me!

When I finish, I'm happy.
It's like winning the lottery.
But then, I remember . . .
I'm supposed to be on a diet.
I now feel so guilty.

Amanda Wilson (13)
Kilkeel High School

Flutter-By

Mossy green, unsightly
Slithering slyly along like an evil snake,
Contentedly, chomping on crisp leaves like a starving man
Gulping down his food.

As the soft snow gently covers the ground, it's gone . . . vanished . . .
Disappeared, never to be seen again!
Time ticks on and on and on . . .
It feels like a lifetime,
Soon Christmas comes, then goes again.

As the sun peeps out from behind the clouds
And the flowers begin to bloom, the end is near.
When the sun sets high in the sky, with a sparkle of magic,
There is the most beautiful creature ever to be seen.

Soon the butterfly is sweeping in and out
Through the trees like a spinning top,
Not a care in the world,
As light as the air.
Mystifying colours and patterns, much better than an art gallery.

The fascinating echo of children laughing
Trying to catch the butterfly.
The centre of every fairy tale.

The mossy green, unsightly caterpillar, is forgotten,
Erased from everybody's mind,
Time is wiped out.
What was once the ugly duckling is now the elegant swan
And the enchanted world of the flutter-by, butterfly has begun.

Gemma Coulter (14)
Kilkeel High School

The Untamed Monster

It had been lurking inside me,
For several days now,
Awaiting the right moment,
To start its prolonged journey.

It started to stir,
Erupting like a volcano deep down inside me,
Spilling out the entire contents of its body,
Like letting acid loose on my agitated stomach.

Slowly but surely, every part of me
Was being savagely ripped apart,
Devoured.

This untamed monster,
Was on the prowl,
It wasn't going to stop,
'Til its prey was totally sabotaged.

Like a fire it raged in the back of my throat,
Guarding the entry to my belly,
Making sure nothing else entered,
To disrupt his fun.

The sensation was toe-curling,
Like nails scraping down a blackboard,
I start to choke,
As though it was sucking my insides out.

That stupid cheesecake,
It set the monster free,
Wouldn't it ever leave me,
Could the damage ever be repaired?

Rebekah Patterson (14)
Kilkeel High School

Car

A grumbling grunt in the distance,
then a side-splitting roar.
The small dot in the distance,
followed by a stream of dust.
It is coming closer and closer,
bigger and bigger,
as if it is chasing.

As I come to a stop
it suddenly shrieks to a halt!
I turn and look,
it furiously growls back at me.
I start to move again.
I hear its paws pounding the ground
as a stream of dust and a brutal roar flies by,
following the beast.

Ben Firth (13)
Kilkeel High School

Happy But Bored

Happiness is the sun shining
Boredom is the rain blocking out the sun.

Happiness is a holiday away from all your problems
Boredom is the end of a holiday and back to work.

Happiness is a day for you
Boredom is a day cleaning up after other people.

Happiness is full of energy
Boredom is tired and going to bed.

Night night.

William Robert Hutchinson (12)
Kilkeel High School

Consuming Death

The staring face of death,
Like a lethal weapon,
At any second ready to kill,
It was so deceiving,
Like a shiny red apple that was rotten inside.
As vile as bubbling sulphur,
As repulsive as decomposed eggs.
I gulped the rotting carcass down.
It was like acid,
Scorching my tongue, blistering my throat,
Corroding me from the inside out.
It was consuming me,
Destruction pumping through my veins.
Sweat was dripping down my face,
My head was spinning,
Images were swirling,
Darkness fell upon me.
My heart was thumping,
I thought it would burst through my chest.
Death's dagger pierces,
Green blood oozes out.
The heart thumping comes to a halt,
Forever.

Rachael Quinn (14)
Kilkeel High School

Chips

C old or warm,
H ard or soft,
I rresistible flavour.
P ut in the oven till they are cooked,
S pecial with sauce.

Naomi Shannon (11)
Kilkeel High School

The Battle Within

The tongue-tingling sensation
Spreads throughout my body,
Slowly creeping down my throat . . .
Until I could feel the burning reach my stomach.
It devours my flesh,
Like a wild, hungry beast.
Slowly eating away
Like maggots at a rotting carcass.
My stomach tries to fight back,
Fervently trying to destroy the intruder.
The battle continues for hours on end -
Who will come out the victor?
My frail body
Begins to show signs of defeat,
Pale and lifeless,
Doubled over in agony
But then the defence makes one final bid for victory,
This time they are victorious
The invaders are soon defeated,
My weakened body begins to recover,
Soon to be back on top form once again,
Daring any other to make an attack.

Leanne Shields (14)
Kilkeel High School

Chips

C rispy and hard,
H ot and crunchy,
I nviting taste,
P otato, soft in the middle,
S ometimes chips smell nice!

David Beck (11)
Kilkeel High School

So Innocent, Yet So Guilty

So innocent, just sitting,
doing nothing.
I picked it up, it felt
so hard and tough
like a piece of steel.
Ate it.
Feeling the tingling down
my throat.
Not knowing that one bite
could cause the consequences
of such an illness.

The next day,
I was as sick as a dog.
It was so flesh-eating
like maggots chewing into me,
corroding like a metal
dissolving in acid.
Bitter like a sour lemon.
So vile,
it was tongue-curdling.

Ruth Shields (14)
Kilkeel High School

The Night Sky

The moon shines down,
spreading a dim light . . .
for miles over the gloomy, dark sea,
along with millions of sprinkled, sparkling stars,
which we are unable to count,
as it looks like a black sheet,
covering all light.
It covers everything a few feet away,
as it gives a sense of blindness.

Darren James Haugh (13)
Kilkeel High School

Untitled

At first I thought she wanted all the attention,
She loved the camera.
She would do and say anything
To get noticed
I mean anything!
Then it all changed.
I somehow saw another side to her.
I looked deeper.
She was just like any normal girl -
With her own feelings.
Even though it's true she loved to be the centre of attention -
This was her life.
It is how she earns a living.
She is intelligent - she knows how to play the crowd.
Now she's got her own identity.
Her *true* identity
Now she is successful.

Grace Maginnis (18)
Kilkeel High School

Peppers!

Peppers come in loads of different colours,
Five colours that are in a rainbow:
Red, orange, yellow, purple and green,
Something that everyone in the world has seen.
They look beautiful and taste delicious.

You don't have to travel far down south,
To find chilli-hot peppers that burn in your mouth.
If you hold your mouth, your ears will steam,
Your eyes will water and will begin to stream.

Laura Smyth (12)
Kilkeel High School

The Stranger

The sounds of laughter echoed through the hall
Everyone was equal
No one would fall
But
As time moved on, so did we,
The feeling of loneliness had slowly taken charge of me
I would never forget, though I wish I could
How she looked upon me
With the utmost contempt
Her anger was silence
And her eyes filled with tears
A stranger I became to her, I could not comprehend
The wounds that separated us would never mend
That's life
All good things must come to an end.

Catherine Orr (17)
Kilkeel High School

Choking On A Chip

Its greasy coating abrasively corroded his throat
as the tongue-tingling chip slothfully slid down!

Like a horse's kick the chip struck his chest,
forcing an agonising splutter!
Gasping for breath, he retched,
compelling it to hurriedly shift into his stomach!

The gut churning effect curdled,
strengthening the scorching pain
which filled his eyes with water.

Coughing profusely he retched again!
The vile, green liquid scorched his throat,
as it surged past and in a magnificent spurt,
came relief.

Paul Maybin (15)
Kilkeel High School

In The Town

I am in the town with my friends
It is the weekend at 10pm, there are:
Chip vans,
Street lights,
Shops,
Pubs,
Cars,
People shouting,
Loud music thumping,
Policemen standing there eating,
Drunk people falling everywhere, singing.
When a car goes past and backfires
This reminds me of a firework going off.
The typical fella who drives these cars:
A show off
With the car done up with new wheels,
Sound system,
The window down with his right hand out
And a fag in his hand,
Seat fully back
And he thinks he is a god.
He has his hair up with gel
His girlfriend has blonde hair and blue eyes.

Alan Robinson (15)
Kilkeel High School

Bananas

Bananas are yellow,
Sometimes with black spots,
They're hard to open
And they're easy to eat.
They taste really nice,
But look a little weird,
You can peel a banana
And it will taste great.

Elizabeth Keown (12)
Kilkeel High School

Betrayal

When I found out
I was so full of rage
Like an annoyed bull ready to attack,
Although I was hurting.
I didn't think she could be so two-faced
Deceitful,
She was supposed to be a friend
Whom I had trusted.
I felt I'd been stabbed in the back.
My eyes filled with tears,
However it wasn't crying I felt like doing,
It was shouting.
My heart was racing,
My palms were sweating.
It seemed as if they were laughing at me
I could imagine the smile on her face.
It was then I saw her for what she really was,
A liar.

Kirsty Morris (14)
Kilkeel High School

Hunting

Never used to like hunting
Then I was given a chance
To shoot a bird.
I loved it after that;
Killed all different kinds
Of animals,
Started hunting with my dogs
The dogs would catch the animal
I was scared at first;
Now I help them to kill.

Terence Huddy (14)
Kilkeel High School

Boredom

Trapped,
In that box of silence.
Time stands still for thirty minutes,
Drawn,
To my multicoloured surroundings,
Observing the variety of expressions and movements:
Tapping,
As a pen repeatedly strikes the table.
Eyes prompting the hands of the clock to move faster.
Glares,
From a superior body at the front of the room.
Chime,
The silence has finally broken,
Finally, freedom!

Linsey Wilson (16)
Kilkeel High School

Heading Out On A Saturday Night

Click, goes the door
I stroll down the road
In the dark cold
Alone.
I hear the trees howling
My hair smells like fresh strawberries.
I walk on, chewing minty gum.
My perfume smells lovely.
I put on my shiny lip gloss
It sparkles like crystals.
I'm getting closer.
Suddenly I hear loud shouting
And the cheering of voices
And the calling of my name.

Lynn Maybin (16)
Kilkeel High School

Everyone's Ocean

My fear struggles to live, begging to breathe,
But I push it under until it dies.
Nothing will fell me, I will not concede,
My feet are rooted in the silky sludge
And I cannot be crushed; I will not stop.
The tide surges against me and I quake,
Wave after wave, they unleash their assault
And as the Earth slams into me I doubt.
But I am safe, the sun is my saviour,
It rises red from the belly of death.
Dawn is breaking, I cannot be sucked back,
Though white horses charge, howling into me.
The force is the moon, it drives them onwards
And it too will bow to the sun's glory.
So stand firm in hope, this world will retreat,
To the trapping jaws of the earthly beast,
Let fear and pain sleep, the sun has risen,
Into the embrace of the perfect Heaven.

David McIlroy (16)
Kilkeel High School

Result!

My eyes turning in my head - the road blurring by.
My stomach wrenched in knots - painfully I sigh
My tongue has swelled - I cannot speak.
My eyes fill up - my legs go weak.
The car door opens - I have to get out.
I feel so dizzy - I wish I could shout.
I get to the doors and they open for me
I cannot go in, 'Don't make me,' my plea.
Everyone is there, standing calm in the light,
I feel quite foolish, how could this be right?
The paper in my hand, I don't know what to do.
I run to the car - not one single U.
Result!

William Nugent (17)
Kilkeel High School

Young Writers - Great Minds From Co Down

Moving On

It was a weird day.
I guess I was walking into school
when it dawned on me.
You could never forget your
first day at school.
The teachers with smiles
from ear to ear,
the classrooms
smelling of fresh paint,
the yelling of the children.
I never thought I would get to
high school.
Children like a crowd of
stampeding bulls
and now the time just seems
to fly.

Claire Johnston (14)
Kilkeel High School

Killowen

We went to Killowen on a trip with the school,
The best thing was the bouldering bit.
We went on a bus with a smell like a farm,
The water we were in was like melted ice.
We walked for a quarter of a mile with our feet in the water
Then it got deeper and we couldn't stand up.
The rocks got higher and the water got shallower.
We climbed over rocks, the bigger, the harder,
We were near the top and the water got deep,
So deep we couldn't swim over and we had to be pulled.
When we got to the top, there was a big cliff
Which we all got to jump off.
The water was deep, about twelve feet,
Then we realised it was time for tea.

Rachel Curran (11)
Kilkeel High School

A Step Into The Unknown

When will safety cease to exist?

Growing older now.
The school's protecting warmth is fading.

I have blossomed and survived
Through wind and storm.
Stayed afloat in a sea of revision.
My leaves are branching out as opportunity opens
Preened every day with such care and time.

Sowing seeds not knowing where
Or if they will develop.
Hoping each seed will sprout into opportunity,
To raise a mighty oak
From such a small acorn as myself.

Hoping my seed of life
Doesn't wither, but continues to flourish
Into a beautiful, blossoming flower.

Kirsty Lewis (17)
Kilkeel High School

Friends

For many years,
We were friends.
Did everything together
Thought it would last,
Until . . .
She betrayed me,
I was devastated
Couldn't believe what she'd done,
Now, we don't talk
We are two strangers.

Kirstie Graham (15)
Kilkeel High School

Friendship

My friends and I were having fun,
Just fooling around with everyone,
Until one night me and my friend
Were in a car flying round some bends.
Car ripped and roared and tumbled over
As if it were a roller coaster,
Then just when things couldn't get worse
The terrible news made me want to burst.
My closest friend was faced with death,
But we're still young, she's full of breath,
This only happens to older people,
Not us, I grabbed my aching shoulder.
I never told her how I felt,
Not even once, now she was dealt
The fact her poor, wee life could end,
I sobbed and held her just to send
A message just to let her know
How much I loved and wanted so,
For her to fight and not give in,
So much for parties, dance and sin,
What was the life and world about?
I watched the tubes and machines in doubt.
I bent my head and prayed and prayed,
'Please God protect, make well,' I said.
She's everything and more to me
And I never told her that you see.
This world is only for a while,
Just has to change - I know that now,
Now I appreciate each day,
Thank God for health and always say,
There is no greater love than this,
The gift of life, oh, what a bliss!

Zoe Nicholson (16)
Kilkeel High School

Getting Ready!

Standing in my bedroom
Clothes on the floor and all around me
One shoe here and one shoe there.
Whatever shall I wear?
Dressing table cluttered
Make-up and hairspray without lids
While I'm getting ready
The music is up full boot
Fast music to get me up and going
Hair takes a long time
Dry it
Heat up straighteners
Get it nice and straight!
Finally, hairspray.

Karen Moore (15)
Kilkeel High School

Nerves

Heart pounded,
Clock ticked,
Nervous,
Jumpy,
Scared,
My heart raced and palms sweated,
Then,
The long awaited noise.
Turned the key,
Heard the rumble,
Did the footwork and gripped the wheel.
With a cold sweat and shaky hands
Carefully selected first,
Checked the reflection and off I went,
I was driving.

Kelly Whyte (17)
Kilkeel High School

Young Writers - Great Minds From Co Down

Looking Back

Finally there after a long day travelling,
I was in Spain!
It was roasting,
As if someone had thrown boiling water around us.
I was full of excitement,
We didn't know what to do first.
Lorraine and I ran straight for the pool,
We didn't even unpack,
Like children in a candy store
The third day came,
It was then I realised
How much I missed home and my friends,
I just wanted to be back home with them.
The rest of the week dragged,
I thought it was never going to end.
Now looking back on my holiday,
I wish I were back there,
It was the best holiday of my life.

Laura Baird (15)
Kilkeel High School

Untitled

On the football pitch
I can see men being tackled,
Ref blowing his whistle
Issuing a yellow card.
Muscles tense and tighten.
I can smell Deep Heat being sprayed
On the injured man.
My mouth is dry
I need a drink.

Matthew Monaghan (15)
Kilkeel High School

Hot Dogs

It looks like an open pencil case,
A short, fat worm in a sleeping bag.
A mouth with a tongue hanging out,
And even a snake in a box.

It has a really warm smell,
The kind that make you say,
'Hooray, hooray, the dinner is ready,
The dinner is ready today!'

If feels like three bumpy waves,
When you slide your fingers across,
A sort of squidgy feeling,
The kind like your teddy bear.

The taste is the most delicious taste
That you will ever enjoy,
The juicy, meaty, porky taste
The kind that tickles my tastebuds.

Mary-Jane McBride (12)
Kilkeel High School

Kids

Rough!
Agony, lots of agony
Pulling each other's hair
Shouting, screaming, yelling
But no one pays any attention
No one even stops to look
Things like ornaments and books
Never sat in their proper place
Fingerprints on the wall, gum on the carpet
I thought to myself, *never again*
To this very day people still ask me,
'Why?'

Donna Morris (14)
Kilkeel High School

It

I looked down at my arms.
Blood flowed from the deep, red scratches
It had attacked me.
I looked to the back seat of the car
Where it was now,
In a cardboard box,
And from it I could hear
Wailing, hissing and scratching.
The lid of the box rose up,
It was trying to escape.
Panicking,
I held the lid down,
Blood from my arm dripping onto the top,
As we made our long journey home.
I lifted the box out of the car.
As the thing moved around inside it,
It rocked from side to side.
I set the box on the floor of the kitchen,
Opened the lid
And stepped back,
It leapt out like a lion onto its prey . . .
A toy mouse.

My new kitten was home.

Julianne Megaw (16)
Kilkeel High School

Spaghetti Bolognese

It's like a mountain of lava
Sliding down my throat.
With worms and snakes tickling me,
As they come out to play.
I can smell the rich flavours,
Mushrooms, mince and onions,
Like they are cooking
On a warm, open fire.

Courtney McClean (11)
Kilkeel High School

The Ulster Museum

Ready to go to Belfast
The bus arrived at the door,
We were on our way to the museum;
We were ready to explore.

The building was very big
And filled with old antiques,
Pottery, bones and mummies;
For archaeologists, some techniques!

We went to the old Egyptian end
And there we saw a real mummy,
Still wrapped up in its old, white cloths;
It didn't look like a dummy.

At last came the gift shop
That was where we went,
To spend some of our money;
But instead it *all* went!

I think the class enjoyed it
And I loved it too,
So if you like history;
This is the place for you!

Laura Agnew (12)
Kilkeel High School

Chicken Kebab

It looks like chopped up wood,
Lumpy and creamy
It looks like a big mountain,
I really love this food.

This food is scrumptious and mouth-watering,
It's like a hot frying pan.
It's roasting, I'd say even better
Than going roller-coasting.

Lisa Newell (11)
Kilkeel High School

Unjustifiable Heartache

The filter has clogged with cynical thoughts,
They overflow in a spate of unbearable, grating nails,
My skull is abraded and solace fails to seep through.
Closing my eyes, I can still see your icy, blue stare;
Constantly darting from my own gaze to my lips.
Such perfect pain is the result of brief pleasure,
Leaving me in an eternity of ambivalence.
Listening to this hectic silence I recall the trundle of wheels,
The soft clopping of hooves and the scent of horses.
They all carry me back to our time.
I see your wave, your understanding nod,
And I recollect the mould of our farewell embrace.
What felt so right is now a distant memory,
And swimming about my mouth,
I find the taste of the sour words, 'What if?'
What if my inhibitions were no obstacle,
And prying eyes looked away?
Ended merely by the calling of our other lives?
If love is such a divine power,
Then distance should be conquered.
Instead we leave each other,
The raw sting of snow spreading on our hearts.
At that time I wish I had seized the moment,
Instead of sharing my regret in this poem.

Andréa Hanna (15)
Kilkeel High School

Strawberry Sherbets

I open my mouth and pop one in,
As it starts to crackle and pop,
Just like a firework in my mouth, it explodes,
As it sizzles like bacon in a pan,
As it fades away like snow when it melts,
As down my throat it goes.

Jourdan Lyons (12)
Kilkeel High School

Death

I feel so empty, so alone
Does anyone feel the same?
Everywhere I look I see the hurt
Feel the anger and the pain.
I want to shout, scream or hurt someone,
Something, hurt myself
It shouldn't have happened! Why did it happen?
Why him? Why now?
Maybe his duty here was fulfilled - he was needed somewhere else -
I will miss him.

Is anyone else hurting? Do they feel pain?
How do they cope with their pain?
It is eating me up inside, until I feel empty.
No life, no soul, nothing, gone.
Will it ever be the same again?
Can we get on with our lives,
Or will we fall into a deep, dark hole?
Where the magic, the life, is drained away.
Here in body, not in mind.
It's over - there's no turning back.

This tragedy has brought some good
Others were saved, given another chance.
It puts life in perspective
We should live life to the full, as if each day's our last,
Like there will be no tomorrow.
As though the end is here
Now!

Laura Wortley (17)
Kilkeel High School

Motorbikes

First time driving
Frightening, exciting, nervous
The bike's revving my reaction
Wind in my hair
First touch of the handles
An aeroplane soaring in the sky
The bikes bond as they drive, flowing together
Zoom, zoom . . .

Katherine Boucher (15)
Kilkeel High School

Speed

Butterflies in my stomach, excitement flowing
Waiting for the bang
My fingers tremble
Engine revving and I click into first
Wheels spinning like a boomerang
Mud falling like rain
The thrills come to an end as the sun goes down.
Speed.

William McKee (15)
Kilkeel High School

Ice Cream

Feels so cold,
You think your fingers will fall off.
As squidgy as a soaking sponge,
Looks like a great big hill,
With a cherry on the top.
It's shaped like a rough sea,
That has not been coloured in,
There are so many flavours,
My mouth waters just thinking about them.

David Pue (11)
Kilkeel High School

Food - Mince And Spuds

This food is like a desert island
Sensational look of a smashing meal
And it is a great meal to eat,
No way is it sweet.

This meal is very soft and squidgy,
It is not *too hot,*
And it is cooked in a pot,
With mouth-watering vegetables included.

This is a lovely food to try,
It is *sensational,*
Absolutely a cracking meal,
In many ways delicious.

Andrew Johnston (12)
Kilkeel High School

Sweets

Oh to the glorious sweet of earth
I can never forget your wonderful taste.
So many types to drool over,
Jelly babies, Haribo and the many types of sherbet.
Shelf by shelf the mountain grows,
Of millions, toffee to the midget gems.
From crunching to sucking,
From licking to picking, still I won't be sick.

I pounce like a leopard to the sweet,
At the sound of every wrapper.
My rotting teeth still won't dissolve,
Or start to go holey and drop to earth.
In all my life the vegetables never passed,
The rotted home in my mouth of old, old me.
I could eat and eat my sweets, sweets, sweets,
Until now where I am sick, *'Urgh!'*

Peter Quinn (12)
Kilkeel High School

Buns

Buns taste great, buns taste good,
They're the most delicious food.
Buns are fun, buns are yum,
They're even nicer in my tum.
I like buns with marshmallow,
I like them deep, not shallow.
Eat them with chocolate or even cream,
You'll like them so much, you'll think it's a dream.

Alice Gordon (12)
Kilkeel High School

Cookie

Cookie, Cookie, you're so sweet;
I once heard of a Cookie mountain.
It was all you could eat.
In the packet you look fine,
In my mouth you are divine.
Cookie, I like it when you're on my lips,
You're better than cherries without the pips.
Your taste beats the rest.

David Holmes (12)
Kilkeel High School

Favourite Foods

The foods that I love the most
Are many, including the Sunday roast.
I love potatoes, pasta and chicken,
I love the flavour they leave in my mouth,
I also love my buns and cake,
Even though they're fatty and bad,
I eat them slowly savouring the taste,
So none of it gets put to waste.

Linda Cargin (15)
Kilkeel High School

Spaghetti Bolognese

It looks like a rushing volcano just waiting
To burst and release its molten lava
It's like worms with mud on top.

It smells like peppers and herbs and more
It's very nice
Mouth-watering, even.

It feels all mushy and gooey
You feel as if it's going
To overflow off your plate.

It tastes spicy,
As if you'd need gallons of water to rinse it down
Its rich aroma just makes you want to stuff your face.

Rebecca McDowell (11)
Kilkeel High School

The Potato

It looks like a lumpy heap of muck,
Or a human brain,
It also looks like a stone
With many eyes.

It feels like a squidgy bit of Playdoh
When it's cooked,
But when it's not cooked
It feels rough and bumpy like a rock.

It tastes like soil if the skin is still on,
It tastes disgusting when raw,
Delicious when cooked,
I love it.

Mark McCullough (11)
Kilkeel High School

Pizza

What I like to eat
Is crunchy and sweet,
It has a red base
As large as your face.

It is hard before cooked,
Go quickly, have a look,
It is scrumptious and yummy,
Straight to my tummy.

You can have ham and cheese,
Or salami and peas,
It's tasty with chips
And leaves sauce on my lips.

This food I eat
Is the best of all,
You get it in packets,
From big to small.

Gemma Teggarty (11)
Kilkeel High School

Curry Chips

They're soft, square, gold and rough,
Runny, lumpy, spicy and hot.
They're all clumped together like a big block,
In a great big dish.
They're long, thin, fat or soft,
They're hard and sticky too.
They've the smell of onions, the smell of sultanas,
All spiced in a lovely canopy of potatoes.
They're hot but still cold.
They're spicy, hot, soft and runny,
Lovely, tasty and lumpy.

Megan Holmes (11)
Kilkeel High School

Chips

They smell like potatoes
And a deep fat fryer
But at the end of the meal
You could eat another
They taste like batter
And make you fatter
They're sort of long
But they do make you strong.

Melissa McConnell (11)
Kilkeel High School

Happiness

H ave a warm feeling in your heart
A re not annoyed with anything
P leased that everyone likes you
P eople think you're fun
I always play with all my friends
N o people make fun of you
E veryone thinks you're funny
S omeone always plays with you
S ome people help you.

Harry Reilly (11)
Kilkeel High School

Emotions

A feeling that everyone has had
N othing can beat it
eX cellent
I have butterflies in my belly
O ur body is full with this emotion
U want to know what is happening
S uspense.

David Henning (12)
Kilkeel High School

Young Writers - Great Minds From Co Down

The Dieter

I stared at the burger sizzling on the grill,
Just thinking about it gave me a thrill.
My mouth watered over its luxurious smell,
My tongue fizzed with excitement
As I pretended to eat it.

It seemed like a week to cook,
It glowed like a rising sun on the plate,
It lay like a huge diamond shimmering,
I had to eat it,
I couldn't resist.

I chomped through the bap and into the meat,
The fat oozed onto my tongue,
Hundreds of explosions erupted into my mouth,
I felt so dirty betraying my diet,
But it felt so good.

Adam Nicholls (14)
Kilkeel High School

Today I Am Sad

Today I am sad,
My life feels so bad.
I lost my best friend,
I hope we can mend.

I want to be happy,
Why can't I be?
I'm going batty,
I want to be me.

Now I'm happy,
Two friends have made up.
She's my best friend again,
And I got a new pup.

Aimee Johnston (11)
Kilkeel High School

The Living Night!

The catseyes shine on a long, winding rkoad,
The sky lights up with twinkling eyes,
There the dragon sneezes,
Leaving behind a bush of burning fire,
The eyes look down on me
As I look out my window at the living night.

The living night is opening more as a Catherine wheel spins,
It's disappearing behind the twinkling eyes,
I jump into my bed and lie,
I shiver while I think about the long, living night.

That night in bed I lie and dream,
The crimson leaves dancing
To the wild wind roving,
I hear a bang!
I jump!
The sky is filled with sparks flying, like a romantic kiss
On a lonesome beach,
Then there is darkness . . . the living night is asleep!

Christine Haugh (13)
Kilkeel High School

Fun

Fun is . . .
Something I feel when I'm doing something I enjoy.
Playing with my mates.
Going to a cinema, or a theme park.
Having one of the best friends in the world.
Going away on holiday.
Playing my favourite video games.
Going to sleep over at a friend's house
Or when they come to your house.

Gregor Strachan (12)
Kilkeel High School

The Fairy

I've found a fairy under my bed
Think it must have come from somewhere far ahead
Because of its sparkling feathers
It must have come from somewhere no one has been
I looked after it carefully, tried feeding her buttercups
Giving her dewdrops to drink and keeping her in the summer sunshine
But it was no good, she was not happy
She looked at me and said I need things you can't provide
I made her a cuddly bed in a shoebox under my bed
But unlike those you've ever heard
But it's out of place here, only if you imagine
And she's growing very well
If you believed in her I would come hurrying to your house
To let you share my wonder
But I won't, instead I will see if you yourself will pass this way.

Laura Campbell (12)
Kilkeel High School

Relief

I can't wait to go to Killowen and get away
From school, work and homework for two whole days.
I want to have good fun instead of being stuck in front of the TV,
I would like to do whatever I please.
I want to go rock climbing and go in a canoe,
Or whatever I would like to do.
It would just be a relief.
What does relief look like, is it big or is it small,
Or is it nothing like that at all?
What colour would relief be - blue black or pink?
Would it smell nice or would it stink?
Will I ever know?

Jake Pulford (12)
Kilkeel High School

Back To School

Back to school once more,
Hope school's not a bore,
Teachers eager to give work,
Pupils dread of homework.

New first years start school,
Hoping they will not be the class fool,
Fifth years under pressure of exams,
Hoping that their knowledge will expand.

School term starts again,
Hoping to win at least one game,
Pupils can't wait to ten past three,
To get out of school and be free.

Amy Bingham (13)
Kilkeel High School

What Is Happiness?

If happiness was a colour
It would be yellow and bright.
If happiness was painted in a picture
It would be such a beautiful sight.

If happiness had a smell
It would smell like a summer flower.
If happiness was in a fight
It would win with its awesome power.

Happiness is a feeling
That lifts your feet off the ground.
Happiness is something
That should definitely be shared around.

Elizabeth Morris (12)
Kilkeel High School

Anger

Is when a person annoys you
When my sister breaks my stuff
When I'm not there
When my parents say I can't go somewhere.

Anger is like a grumpy lion
It makes your face turn red
Anger would be better off staying in bed.

Robert Tomkins (11)
Kilkeel High School

Chips

Floury chips, yummy, scrumptious
Smells delicious
Tasty out of the oven
Soft and smooth in my mouth like silk
A golden sun
And a crispy outside like a layer of crisp
I feel excited like an aeroplane
My tummy rumbles like an earthquake.

Andrew Wilson (11)
Kilkeel High School

Our World

The world doesn't beat
To the sound of just one drum
What might be right for you
May not be right for some
A man is born
With a gun in his hand
And from every day since
He's been fighting for our land.

Richard McKee (15)
Kilkeel High School

Pizza!

Pizza is nice,
Pizza is food,
Pizza can fill you
With stuff that's good.

Pizza is different,
All toppings you can get,
All different colours,
The nicest you've met.

Pizza is wonderful,
Pizza Hut's the best,
Cheese drips everywhere
And dirties your vest.

Pizza is nice,
Pizza is food,
Pizza's the best,
So eat it, it's good!

Alex Speers (13)
Kilkeel High School

Chew, Chew

I'll always love chewing gum
I've got plenty, here, do you want some?
Berry, apple, lemon or lime?
Slurp, slurp, slurp to teachers it's a crime
Keep blowing bubbles
And you'll have no troubles
Unless it's in your hair
You'll be crying, 'It's not fair!'
Mountain fresh, cool breeze
If you don't take some
Your mouth will freeze
Fruity flavours are flowing down
When it is around I cannot frown.

Nicola Bell (12)
Kilkeel High School

Chicken

It can be very delicious
When it's nice and spicy
When it's from the 'Country Fried' it's scrumptious
Or with your Sunday dinner it's juicy
So eat some chicken that's luscious
Chicken, chicken, you're so fine
Chicken, chicken you're divine
So let me chomp your wing and leg.

Ashley Cracknell (13)
Kilkeel High School

Cabbages

Cabbages are yummy,
They are good for your tummy;
Cabbages grow in the ground,
You can buy them for a pound.

Cabbages are nutritious,
They are also delicious;
Cabbages are green,
They are not heard but sometimes they are seen.

Emma Connor (12)
Kilkeel High School

Ice Cream

A smooth, creamy taste in my mouth will flow,
The shivers run over me from my head to my toe.
Colours may vary from brown to white,
To everyone around it's a mouth-watering sight.
To finish it off are your own little dips,
So magnificent, so glorious, when it first touches your lips.

Michelle Skillen (12)
Kilkeel High School

The Moon's Dazzle

The moon gleams over the sea,
Looking at the boats pass the flash of light.
It is so exquisite,
Looking at the waves,
Swaying side-to-side like a push of a swing,
Splish-splashing against the high walls and tall boats.

The moon shines upon me,
When I'm in my bed,
It almost blinds me with its dazzle.
The wind chimes mirror a glow of light.

The moon glows on every house in the neighbourhood,
It looks like a long, thick pencil put on fire.
It hypnotises all the children asleep with its beauty.

The moon also shimmers on the swing park,
I can hear the swings squeaking and creaking,
Rocking backwards and forwards,
Like the rock of a baby's cradle,
Suddenly I fall asleep,
With the noises of human footsteps.

Kerri Elizabeth Graham (13)
Kilkeel High School

Sweetcorn

S weet and healthy
W arm and yummy
E arly or late
E verywhere it grows
T aste the butter
C urly on top
O pen the leaves
R eady to cook
N ever left on my plate.

Lesley Gordon (11)
Kilkeel High School

Young Writers - Great Minds From Co Down

Belladonna

Down she slipped,
Starting her turmoil and destruction.
Tunnelling between the walls,
Causing choking,
Just like a piece of string,
Tightening around the oesophagus.

Reaching her destination,
She began gnawing away,
Like an army of ants,
Consuming a discarded rotting lettuce.
The contamination began.
The toxic, vile, curdling, acidic taste
Singed and scorched my tongue.
The sizzling and hissing
Was screaming in my brain.

The sign of the skull and crossbones
Was imprinted before my eyes,
Revealing the belated warning.
Darkness and deadly deceit
Made me collapse to my knees.
Down,
Down I slumped.
I surrendered.
The deterioration was almost complete.

Jane Annett (14)
Kilkeel High School

Roller Coaster

Scary, exciting, my heart was racing,
It went silent,
I slowly came to the big drop,
Suddenly it fell
Like a speeding car
As it came to an end.
Excellent.

Wendy Hanna (15)
Kilkeel High School

The Unicorn

I've found a unicorn in the forest.
I think it must have come from a secret island,
Because it was covered with sand.

I looked after it well,
Tried to break it in so I could ride it,
But it became scared, as if to say,
'I need something you can't provide.'

I made it get its confidence back,
Not unlike some other people would do,
But it's out of place here,
So I'll send it back and
Hope it will be happy in a different place.

If you believed in it,
I would come hurrying to your house
To let you share my wonder,
But I want instead to see
If you will pass this way.

Lauren Baird (12)
Kilkeel High School

Chips

I really have to say
I could eat chips every day.

If I have chips for dinner
I know they'll be a winner.

Brown sauce, red sauce, vinegar and salt
With these on my chips there won't be a fault.

When I go into Dianne's
She will make me chips from the frying pans.

With my chips I make a chip butty
I know that I will go plain nutty.

Julie Annett (13)
Kilkeel High School

The Cliff

We were on holiday and decided to go for
A cliff walk.
The sky was grey and full of clouds
It fitted my mood.
We began to walk along the path
Which led to the cliff.
The stones scraped against my ankles
The path grew thinner.
No railings,
No security,
No safety.
One wrong foot . . .
I would see my watery grave.
The waves crashed down against the rocks,
The sun escaped from the clouds
It spilled its rays over the sea
We reached the end
At first I hated the idea of climbing a cliff -
But the view changed my mind -
It was gorgeous.

Jennifer McConnell (14)
Kilkeel High School

Potatoes

They look like the ground
On the planet Mars
They feel like a fat, rough stone
They taste like chips
And smell like them too
They look like a good old vegetable
Lovely, sweet, old, magic inside
When the magic is released you will feel it
And you will be basking in the glorious taste.

Euan McCracken (12)
Kilkeel High School

Chocolate

I slowly open the wrapper
Revealing a lovely treasure,
I break off a chunk,
My mouth waters
As I slowly place it in.
It starts to melt
And so do I,
The taste fills my mouth
Like a smooth, scrumptious river,
Flowing down my throat.
It's there, then suddenly vanishes!
Piece by piece, I eat the lot.
The desire for it is too great,
I just eat and eat,
Till all I have left, is the wrapper.

Emma Tremlett (13)
Kilkeel High School

Potatoes!

Potatoes are the only veg
I won't eat,
Because the smell reminds me of
An old man's feet.

Their skin looks like a diseased man
With an old, wrinkly head,
Who's halfway up to Heaven,
Nearly dead.

The taste in my mouth
Makes me wanna puke,
It's just warm mush,
I think it's worse than the look.

Kathy Newell (13)
Kilkeel High School

Poison

The pungent liquor swirled round
Making me dizzy.
It churned in my stomach
Intoxicating my body.

The tongue tingling taste
Felt like jumping beans,
My body was numb . . .
Growing more infectious.

It choked me and
Hissed angrily like a venomous snake going for the kill.
The lethal poison stabbed me like a ton of icy daggers.
The burning sensation flowed through my body,
Deteriorating my skin.

It corroded through my brittle bones like a vicious chainsaw
Ripping up decayed wood.
My stomach was a butter churn,
Making me violently sick.

I looked again,
Wearily.
The fiery red substance shimmered in the light.
The skull and crossbones had warned me.

Agony boiled in my blood.

I fell,
Down
And down
Into the pool of the toxic liquid.

Sandra Baird (14)
Kilkeel High School

Sunrise

I watched it creeping like a lion,
Slowly and silently,
Over streams and mountains,
Round trees and houses.
It gained on the fleeing darkness,
Overtaking it and surging through the land.
It raised its sleepy head,
Checking to see that night had left,
That the stars were gone,
And the sky was empty.
The face slowly brightening,
The day had begun.
Shaking that weary head,
It sent beams of happiness in all directions,
Those beams were so wonderful,
That they started the birds to sing,
And the flowers to wake.
Now in full swing,
All were blinded by its beauty.
Shining for all it was worth,
It brought grins to people's faces,
Even the oldest, ugliest tree,
Is radiant in its presence.
Nothing,
Not even the most amazing rainbow
Can compare to an early morning sunrise.
The sight of sun,
Could bring tears to your eyes.
It really is
The most beautiful thing in the world.

Lynette McCavery (13)
Kilkeel High School

Fluff

Contradictory creature
From the corner of my eye
I see it crawling along the ground
Not a sound.
I tried to grab it
But it slipped through my hand like a bar of soap.

I looked down
I could see two big eyes looking back,
As if to say, 'Please don't kill me.'
I lifted it up into my hand,
As it struggled to escape.

It was so fluffy and furry,
And had lots of feathery legs.
It was so horrible, the shivers ran down my spine,
I let it go as it tickled my hand,
And it blew away.

Nadine McConnell (13)
Kilkeel High School

Roaring Waves

The lion charged towards me
like a bullet from a gun.
It got bigger and bigger
Its growls got louder and louder
My heart pounded faster and faster.
Its eyes looked straight at me,
It suddenly stumbled
and crashed at my feet.
My heart stopped pounding.
I waited for another.

I looked in the distance.

Jenny Cunningham (13)
Kilkeel High School

Submarines

In murky waters, fish swim,
They live in the sea.
Bubbles scream and try to escape
to the surface, freedom.

Travelling in secret areas,
In search of prey,
Like a magnet and metal
sharks are attracted to the
danger and power of the mighty engine.

Proximity brings rumbling
of this abominable beast
on the move towards another land.

Amy Dodds (13)
Kilkeel High School

Army Animal

The cheetah crawled through the long grass,
His camouflage concealed him.
He stopped . . .
Scanned the surrounding area . . .
And continued on.

He stopped again,
. . . He'd spotted it.
He slipped through the waving Celtic supporters,
Not daring to breathe . . .
Then suddenly . . . he pounced.

Adrian McCullough (13)
Kilkeel High School

Young Writers - Great Minds From Co Down

Hunting

Excitement, waiting, drama, watching,
listening for sound of the horn
to be blown, completely still and silent.

And we're off, like a band of racehorses speeding
down an open track, clearing every
fence or hurdle that comes at us.

The bloodthirsty hounds chasing its
scared, innocent and death-doomed prey,
trapped like a cat chasing a
frightened heart-racing mouse.

Like hunters we're endlessly
alert, anxious and awake,
scanning each area for movement,
chasing your own, every heartbeat races.

Diane Graham (15)
Kilkeel High School

First Football Match

Nervous but filled with fury,
Chants get louder,
Furious voices erupt in the sky,
My heart pumps like a train
Getting faster and faster
Crowd cajoles and crushes,
Tense excitement,
Elation.

Jonathan McCulla (15)
Kilkeel High School

Poisonous Pleasure

That first bite, melting in your mouth,
a warm glow
as it carefully caresses your throat,
a sensatiion of satisfaction and fullness,
the stomach starts to ease.

The passion for food fades,
the body distinguishes the vile,
putrid disease,
that surges around the bloodstream.

Piercing my delicate insides like a rusty dagger,
it pulses through my veins,
intoxicating my feeble body.

Insomnia sets in and the eyesight goes,
colours become blurred and drums . . .
start to beat against the insides of . . .
my ghoulish grey skull.

Streaks of red thunder scratch
my eyes,
cold beads of sweat trickle . ..
diagonally down my pale skin.
As I lie in morbid pain,
my stomach fights a battle
never ending,
like a soldier doomed
to die in battle.

Sarah Graham (15)
Kilkeel High School

Decisions

'Yes' or 'No?'
It's always there,
In my dreams, my classes, my thoughts.
Why can't I decide?

If a decision was made it would
Disappear.
Or would I be left with a fear,
A fear of the unknown?

So many places, forms, information,
My brain is going to explode!
I can't take any more,
I need to escape reality.

Anything is better than in-between.
Black or white,
Not a dull, gloomy shade of grey.
Now, I am coloured every shade of grey.

Everything is so straightforward to an innocent mind.
My decision would be made.
If I was older there would be no choice,
Only a chance to reflect.

What is it I am afraid of?
University, school, the future?
Or simply
A missed opportunity?

Leanne Newell (17)
Kilkeel High School

Ogre

O ld and scary
G reen and hairy
R ed eyes and big ears
E ats anything.

Kirk Whyte
Kilkeel High School

Flawless

Isn't she lovely with her warm smile
Blonde locks
Her quaint little eyes
Her rosy cheeks
The way she starts her daily gossip session
With a gentle nudge
A purposefully lowered head
Turns out
The person I thought she was
Could turn out to be anybody
Like that person crossing the street
Or drinking coffee in the café
Or cradling a child . . .
Her delicate features scrunched into sheer determination
As she forced the door open
She left a trail of unspoken words
Screaming at me in her wake
As she sought refuge among my friends
My friends
I mourn her as a lost friend
Who knows
Maybe we'll meet again one day as we
Cross the street . . . cradle a child . . . or drink our coffee.

Rachael Bleakley (17)
Kilkeel High School

Roller Coaster

Pouncing, pulsating heart, churning stomach.
The steps shuddered like legs knocking together.
Sitting waiting, help! My belt won't fasten!
Help comes, my plan to get off doesn't work
Motion, movement,
Fear.

Sara Holmes (15)
Kilkeel High School

Tempting Death

Temptation . . .
Like a rose waiting to be picked
Stabbing me!
Thorns piercing my skin,
Slipping into my body,
Like a venomous snake creeping,
Silently gaining on its prey.
Taste buds tremble!
Sourness squatting in my mouth,
As vile as rotten flesh,
Tearing down my throat,
Gnawing at my flesh.
Grabbing me!
Breathless . . .
Choking as if I were drowning.
Trapped!
Heaving, wretching,
Sweat . . .
A steady flow,
A river with a plentiful source.
Sparks!
All ablaze!
Burning within me
Like the hidden depths of Hell.

Kathryn McCullough (14)
Kilkeel High School

My Brother

Jealousy and hatred
filled my body.
Brother was born,
staring straight through me,
as if he saw the truth.
Unnatural guilt of loneliness.
Always regret.

Laura Annett (15)
Kilkeel High School

That's Not Funny

Am I the problem,or is it you?
Because I'm confused!
Always laughing and joking together
You made me learn, I love to argue,
It gives me satisfation
It's just funny
Someone so sure can doubt
You used to agree
Then you became weird:
You changed!
That's not funny!
It's just a joke!
What's with that stare?
Am I supposed to choke?
Since when did you get so judgmental,
So moral?
Clearly a joke!
Why aren't you laughing?
Do you think we're a shining moral example?
Who are you trying to impress?
Fine! Stop enjoying yourself
'Cause I'm determined you won't spil my fun
As I laugh in response:
'Yes it is!'
Oh look - others laugh too,
What? I'm not laughing at you!
Get over yourself - you look stupid!
Nobody is trying to be like you!
So have fun - we won't judge!
Do you understand?
You're no example of morals . . .
You're judging now!
I'm trying to make you learn,
That this 'fake' you -
That's not funny!

Deborah Hanna (18)
Kilkeel High School

My One True Friend

A kind and considerate friend had I,
until one day it stopped.
She had changed but
I did not.
There was she; perfect, untouchable, superior.
Yet all I had was loneliness, isolation; I was
inferior.
Power was now her friend, with the world
suspended in her hand.
After all, this was what she had planned.
My trust had been abused,
how could I have been such an innocent fool?
Now I crouch beneath her shadow,
with faded memories of the friend I used to follow.

Emma Teggarty (17)
Kilkeel High School

The Sea

I look out at the sea,
It is so still and blue,
But nearer to the coastline,
The waves, there are a few.

The sand it is a-changing,
From pale to darker brown,
And the pebbles, they get wetter,
I can hear the swishing sound.

The seabirds, some are flying,
While others sit and rest,
They seem to be enjoying
Their ride upon the crest.

Warren Nugent (13)
Kilkeel High School

Tennis

Gentle breeze, blinding sun,
The game begins!
A thunderous serve!
Racing steps pound the court,
A small green missile flies over the net,
Smack, smack and *smack* again,
Ball whizzing this way and that,
Changing shape, changing size,
Back and forth,
Pace changes,
Ball floats,
Smash!
Crashes the net!
Ball's dead!

Mark Stevenson (15)
Kilkeel High School

High School

First day into high school.
My head was throbbing with worries.
It was going to be like a prison.
Torturous homework and teachers like demons.
The school would be like a maze.
I'd need a map to get around,
But my thoughts were wrong.
It was like a well-signed road,
You knew exactly where to go.
Homework was a breeze
And most teachers were angels
. . . that first day!

Mark Campbell (15)
Kilkeel High School

My Invisible Friend

When everyone is gone
You've always been there,
You were at the zoo, the beach,
The park, the trip to nowhere.

Of course, I was just six then,
But you never let me forget you,
Did you? Remember,
It was always me and you!

You've always been a laugh
And had such crazy ideas.
But that one time you went too far,
You brought me to tears.

You left after that, didn't you?
Where did you go? Then it hit me,
And what more can I say?
The realism of your invisibility
Still haunts me to this day.

Leonora Hanna (17)
Kilkeel High School

Betrayal

Isolated, lonely, betrayed, angered,
Few of the ways I was made to feel,
Supposed to be a 'true' friend, but I simply
Wanted to push her bitter intentions aside,
To scream, rant and rave, as if
I had just been declared bankrupt.
'I felt like it,' was my reply,
How could she do this?
My mouth filled with the taste of disgust,
I could never put my trust in her again,
Her sourness still lingers close by,
Forgiveness walks away in the distance.

Lauren Fitzpatrick (17)
Kilkeel High School

Demolition Day

I took my first bite of the deadly substance,
Not knowing what I had let myself in for.
I felt a burning sensation flood the lining of my mouth
Like a jellyfish brushing its stinging tentacles against me.
As I swallowed, my tongue dissolved the rotten slime
As rapidly as a deceased hand plunged into acid.
It forced its way down,
Down,
Down,
Tearing and ripping apart everything
That dared to cross its path.
I felt an explosion in my stomach,
Like a dormant volcano just waiting to erupt.
It tore away my organs like a dog
Ravenously chewing a bone,
Completely obliterating my insides,
Leaving nothing left to salvage.
A foul stench filled the kitchen,
Nauseating me.
As I hurried away from it, I realised
That my cramps and twinges were gone,
Forgotten,
And would definitely not be missed.

Lauren Elder (15)
Kilkeel High School

Fantasy

His soft, dark hair
Brushing against my face,
His arms wrapped around
Cuddling me!
Two seconds later . . .
. . . He was gone.
I felt so

Special!

Diane Curran (14)
Kilkeel High School

Winter

Dark and gloomy weather came,
The swallows fled with fright.
Trees all stripped like skeletons,
With their leaves all tumbled off.
The ditches now stand bare, stripped of their cover.
The clouds have cruelly choked the sun,
The howling wind cuts through the air,
Killing the summer heat.
Poor poppies now dead,
Falling to the ground and buried in snow.
This winter has crept up like a cat upon a mouse,
This time the cat seems to have had a victory.

The tall mountains stand
Like snowballs ready to roll.
They watch over our emerald land, lost in the snow
And the rough sea beyond.
Where towering waves beat down upon the rocks,
The mountains are deserted.
The freezing sheep have all gone home,
All that's left now is a white sheet,
And icy rivers washing around the mountain's cold feet.

Steven Baird (13)
Kilkeel High School

Smarties Bar

Just thinking of a Smarties bar,
Makes your mind drift very far.
All those Smarties dipped in white,
Everyone knows the taste is a delight.
Into 'Graham's Ice Cream' I go,
To make my mouth overflow.
It feels like a rainbow in my mouth,
All my slabbers are falling south.
Of all the bars I ever ate,
You're the one I won't forget.

Jayne Annett (13)
Kilkeel High School

176   *Young Writers - Great Minds From Co Down*

Chocolate

My fantasy food is chocolate,
Creamy, dreamy chocolate.
Mouth watering chocolate,
All day, all night.
Please, just one small bite.
I really wish I had some chocolate,
Just so that I can taste the taste
Of creamy, dreamy chocolate.
Too much to get,
Too much to taste.
What shall I get?
No time to waste,
Too much to choose,
Too much to see -
I think I'll go with Cadbury's.

Nicole Murphy (13)
Kilkeel High School

Basketball

The sound of the basketball bouncing
Like a machine gun in a war,
The crowd cheering you on,
The sight of the basket floating through the hoop.
Accelerating feeling of scoring
A three pointer or slam dunk,
Soaring through the air to score,
The hooter when someone scores
Like a fog horn.
The size of the players -
Giants of six foot five inches or more
Tall and incredible athletes
Aren't they . . . ?

Mark Burden (14)
Kilkeel High School

Freedom

The night is still,
The navy-blue sky is alight with stars,
twinkling ecstatically, as the moon sits alone.
Alone . . . like me.
Huge, white, odd, depressed - *different!*
The moon can't escape . . . but I can!

Bang! a gunshot echoes in the distance,
They're coming!
I leap up, my heart lurches.
I bolt through the trees, their arms pointing
which way I should go.
I'm a cricket-light on my feet, jumping, dodging;
No! They're getting close.
I can't let them get me!
My heart's thumping - I can see the edge of the forest.
Run! Run! Don't give up!
One more step . . . bang!

A searing pain takes a firm grasp of my leg,
It travels slowly all the way up my stunned body.
I wretch and wriggle in pain.
I'm *not* going back to that living Hell - no matter what!

I grab at the leaves and roots, pulling myself across the ground.
I've reached the river bank!
Plunging in, I know the icy water will carry me to safety.

I grin to myself,
Their zoo will just have to be . . .
Polar bare!

Sara Russell (13)
Kilkeel High School

Chips

All the chips are mine,
I eat them all the time.
I love them fat or thin,
Not one goes in the bin.

Chips are great food,
They put me in a good mood.
Please don't waste
The goodness of the taste.

I love them long, short
Chips are so *my sort!*
I love them when I'm mad
And even when I'm bad.

Rebekah Campbell (13)
Kilkeel High School

Untitled

Babies crying, people talking and
Never knowing when to shut up!
Air hostesses pushing those noisy trolleys past you,
With the smell of the disgusting food that made me vomit.
The feel of the rough, prickly walls as we walked down the tunnel.
Holding on to my hand luggage as tightly as I can.
Scared stiff!
Gasping to get the last breath
Before I entered the dreaded aeroplane.
I hate it so much!

Natashia McCullough (15)
Kilkeel High School

Chocolate

Chocolate can represent many a person's dream,
It melts in your mouth as though it's cream.
There is dark, plain or white to fulfil your desire,
There is peanut, nougat even bubbly to admire,
When you place it on your tongue, the velvety taste,
Inspires all mankind, a piece not to waste.

Christopher Maguire (12)
Kilkeel High School

Chinese

C heer up! Tonight is the night,
H ave a Chinese and relax,
'I t has to be sweet and sour,' I said!
N othing else will do.
E verybody loves it
S weet and sour for me again, please.
E very weekend, deserves one.

Diane Rooney (15)
Kilkeel High School

Burger

B ig
U nbelievable
R ound
G rilled
E xcellent
R eal beef.

Geoffrey McConnell (14)
Kilkeel High School

Candyfloss

To me candyfloss is the most tasty food,
It's all different colours, maybe even the colours of the rainbow.
As soon as you set the tiniest bit on your tongue
Your eyes start to water.
Your taste buds jump with excitement, shouting, *'More! More!'*
Your mouth starts to dribble,
It's so soft and fluffy, like a bunny's tail.
You can see the sugar sparkling, calling, *'Eat me!'*
It's so sticky but irresistible.
You can't resist the sensation.
Your mouth is saying, 'I want more!'
You take more and more and more
Until . . . there is nothing left in the packet . . .
Your dream is over!

Jemma McKee (12)
Kilkeel High School

The Night Heat

The wind was like a fan,
destroying the terrible heat,
quenching me
for a drop of cool, refreshing water
in the soothing pain.

In the dark, deafening night,
as you walk from here to there.
It makes you want to collapse
with the powerful force,
of gravity.

Stefan Johnston (13)
Kilkeel High School

Young Writers - Great Minds From Co Down

Chocolate

Chocolate, I cannot do without
Take a bite and know without a doubt
That I love this mouth-watering junk,
More than a big, strong, muscly hunk.
Oh I just adore the temptation,
Of this wonderful, delicious sensation,
That satisfies me, time after time.

It makes me happy when I'm sad,
Gloomy or just feeling bad.
Cheap, not expensive,
Scrumptious, not repulsive
It's like it's from above,
Where the place is full of love.
Yes, it's Heaven! Heaven! Heaven!

Its smoothness is so delicate,
It always looks so elegant.
Comes in all shapes and sizes,
Dark, white, milk, I'll surprise you!
My craving for it is there, eternally,
My wanting is everlasting,
For my tempting, luscious chocolate.

Its company is truly pleasurable,
Lustful and indeed so desirable.
My only necessity in life
Is to have it without strife.
Oh I want it,
Oh I love it,
Please, I need my chocolate.

Samantha Woollard (12)
Kilkeel High School

Christmas Dinner

C hewy
H uge
R ough
I ntense
S teamy
T asty
M outh-watering
A wesome
S avoury

D elicious
I nteresting
N ice
N oel
E normous
R avishing.

Alan Burden (13)
Kilkeel High School

Food

Chick curry
Rice
Spare ribs
Mild and steaming
Served on a plate.
Coke to wash it down,
Muffins and pink custard.
Eat till I'm full.

Kristofor Fitzpatrick (16)
Kilkeel High School

Granny

14 Bignian Avenue,
The focus of my week.
As Tuesday follows Monday
My dinner is always there.
Each day at four, without fail,
Roast beef, potatoes and two veg.
Granny is the mainstay,
A cook, a guide and friend.

Niall McMurray (16)
Kilkeel High School

Succeed Or Fail?

Excitement, fear
I didn't know if I was going to succeed or fail,
I put my foot on the board
I rolled up to the steps.
I felt like an eagle soaring.
Board spinning below my feet.
My feet catch it,
Success!

John Knox (15)
Kilkeel High School

New Pupil

Fire, excitement
Like a scared fox evading its captors,
My heart stops
The first steps are taken.
I cannot go back,
Everything goes numb.
It's time I conquered this fear.
No time to be nervous now.

Andrew McCoy (15)
Kilkeel High School

The Dieter

I ordered it . . .
I knew it would be hard to resist!
It came . . .
My diet, I thought it needed rewarding,
It was over!
I took a bite,
My tongue felt like it had thrown a party,
It was fantastic!
'Stuff the diet,' I said.
I felt like I had starved for days,
Weeks, months.
I want more -
I can't resist it
Yummy, scrumptious, delicious,
Everything I see is so tempting.

Zara Chambers (13)
Kilkeel High School

The Menu

The priceless flavour of succulent roast chicken
Like the smell of a Sunday dinner
Being cooked.

The majestic flavour of mushrooms
In a thick creamy sauce
Which tickles my tastebuds and leaves them
Quite tantalised.

Potatoes, light as air and fluffy as
The tops of a cauliflower
Mixed in
With my steaming hot vegetables.

Elaine Wackett (16)
Kilkeel High School

Young Writers - Great Minds From Co Down

Burger

B ig
U nreal
R ound
G orgeous
E xcellent
R eal beef.

Harold Robinson (13)
Kilkeel High School

Dreams

Dreams can come true
If you take the time to
Think about what you want.
Find out who you are;
Be honest with yourself.
Find out what is important for you,
Find out what you are good at.
Don't be afraid to make mistakes,
Work hard to achieve your targets,
When things are going wrong
Don't give up - work harder!

Michelle Burns (15)
Kilkeel High School

Turkey

T asty
U nsalted
R oasted
K ebab
E xcellent with stuffing
Y ummy!

Mark Annett (13)
Kilkeel High School

Teachers

They're mostly disliked,
Boring and repetitive.
Going on and on and on
And on . . .
Forced to learn lots
And lots of information.
Looks and sounds like total trash to some,
Bang! Our brain explodes,
Just too much to handle.
They're usually ugly, like big crocodiles,
Their big eyes watching you, staring you down.
Lifeless, they often seem to be,
Sitting at their desk, doing nothing, saying nothing
School's just that little bit harder,
Seeing it's already hard enough to endure.
Sigh!

Ricky Hanna (13)
Kilkeel High School

Sausages

The succulent taste
There is no waste,
Laughing and crying
Stopping and buying.
Using your money
Not to buy honey!
The form and shape
Sitting all rolled up in tape.
They're one of my favourite dinners
On my plate, they're always a winner.

Sarah-Jayne Annett (13)
Kilkeel High School

Another Day

Tick, tick, tick,
Brrring!
The clock goes off,
I wake up to face another day.
My head throbs,
Thoughts come rushing through my mind.
I pull the sheets up around me, snug and warm.
I can't get out of bed,
I can't face another day.
I lie in bed awake,
Hands on the clock keep moving.
I put on a brave face
And haul myself out of bed.
I look in the mirror,
My eyes puffy and red.
I pour myself some juice,
Tears run down my cheek and into the glass.
I can't face another day.
How can I survive?
Granny's died,
Gone.

Amy McKee (11)
Kilkeel High School

Chocolate . . .

Galaxy, Dairy Milk and Belgian too,
A relaxing taste for me and you.

Chocolate eclairs and chocolate cake,
Which of these would you rather take?

Chocolate buns, chocolate Smarties,
Even chocolate fingers for parties.

Chocolate ice cream, chocolate wafers,
Have I got any takers?

Claire Annett (12)
Kilkeel High School

Young Writers - Great Minds From Co Down

Sweets

Sweets, glorious sweets,
So enjoyable to eat.
Soft ones, hard ones, chocolate ones too,
Some for me and some for you.

I can never decide which one to pick,
Sadly too many may make us sick.
Last time we ate one after another,
And boy didn't we get into bother!

My mum was so mad
That she told my dad.
He shouted, 'No more sweets, straight to bed,'
And off we scrambled, as his face got red.

So now we have a midnight feast,
Once or twice a year at least,
And Mum and Dad, they never know,
About the cramps down below.

Brush your teeth at least twice a day,
And eat less sweets or you will pay.
Filling after filling is not much fun,
As the dentist approaches with his drill gun.

We've learned to listen before it's too late
Dentures floating in a glass, that I would hate.
Less sweets eaten and more brushing done,
Or raw gums and PoliGrip will be next to come!

The moral of this story, it has to be said
No more eating of sweets in bed
And listen to our elders, who seem to know it all,
But it's either that or out our teeth will fall.

Louise McConnell (12)
Kilkeel High School

Forever Gone

He creeps in out of nowhere,
Prowling on his prey.
Crash!
He devours all in his way,
Distress.
He makes you feel broken, empty, destroyed.
The morning after,
The land looks barren.
No life appears to move.
The raven's harsh call
Pierces the hearts
Of those who have lost things
That mean the most to them.
There's no going back,
Gone forever.

Judith Cherry (16)
Kilkeel High School

Chocolate

Crispy or Crunchie, give me some Munchies
Soft or hard so long as it's not lard.
The scrumptious taste, pastes your tongue,
Stop tempting me please, I want chocolate not cheese.
My wishes come true, when I eat you.
Snickers, Crunchie or Mars, I love all those bars,
For a tasty treat on a cold night,
Hot chocolate tastes just right,
It melts in your mouth, soft and delicious
When I eat you, you fill all my wishes.

Stacey Hanna (12)
Kilkeel High School

Ode To Chilli Con Carne

Oh how I love chilli con carne,
You drive me so barmy.
You are hot and spicy, like an inferno,
When I eat you I say, 'I need water, *now!*'

With your spicy sauces and soft rice,
You know you taste more than nice.
Your chilli powder is the key
To why I'm so addicted to thee.

My tongue is on fire,
You are so delicious,
When I eat you
You fulfil my wishes.

Rachel Hanna (13)
Kilkeel High School

Travelling Train

It starts to go very fast,
Slithering across the ground.
Going to its next stop,
Winding around the trees and rivers.
Always on the look out
Colourful designs on the top.
Long, thin body out
With its eyes so bright so it can see
A track to go across.
On the prowl for prey,
To lead them on for another day.
Screeches when it stops,
On the rails, like a snake hissing
Continuously at its prey.

Christopher Teggarty (13)
Kilkeel High School

Cotton Wool

It's white and fluffy as it whizzes in the whooshing wind,
Soaring left and right.
With its different shapes and sizes
As if someone has separated it or took a big bite.
It leaves detached ends.
Someone might say it is bundles of soft snow,
You could reach out and throw.
They could be stretched and stretched
Until they rip down the middle.
Eventually they fill up with water and then explode.
The water lashes down,
Splish, splash!

Rachel McConnell (14)
Kilkeel High School

A White Rose

With clouds like leaves,
they moved apart
to reveal its splendour.
With its glowing, white face,
it lit up the night sky.

With the wind blowing gently,
it drifted.
Slowly moving along,
never fading.
Even when the rain set in,
its light shone on!

Samantha Hanna (13)
Kilkeel High School

Alarm Clock

The world stops . . .
It crows, 'Cock-a-doodle-do!'
As I look, I see the cockerel,
It looks up for some seed, nothing is there.
It crows again, 'Cock-a-doodle-do!'

He comes and clatters his tin whilst chattering
To the rooster.
It pecks, it eats and stops for a breath.
It crows, 'Cock-a-doodle-do!'
Until the night falls.

Philip Edgar (13)
Kilkeel High School

Act Of Kindness

A flash in the distance, illuminating the sky,
Revealing dark intentions, a darkening shape,
Invading human minds, making them comatose but audible,
And they like it, the further they get out.
A flash of hope, sending sparks which light up
The darkest corners of the soul.
As the flash and sparks die, once again,
So does the heart.
Hatred floods back, hardening it.
Another flash, bigger than the last,
Begins to thaw the icy regions of the mind.

Matthew Forsythe (13)
Kilkeel High School

Yo-Yo

The exhilarating feeling of letting go
That daring jump, free from blame.
Plummeting through the air, boldly,
Like a bird ready to dive into the ocean.
The existence of the Earth, flashing towards him
Plunging forward and spinning randomly.
Suddenly a jerk of hope and a sense of euphoria
Spiralling back up, to grasp the hand of
The one you know.
Overwhelmed with accomplishment
And feeling blithesome.

Chloe Johnston (14)
Kilkeel High School

Hideous Pride

I thought it was extinct
Though I was wrong!
The red hill was back
But this time there was
Nothing to stop it!

Its walls grew higher and stronger,
As I got closer, it started to rumble.
The red hill exploded,
It squirted right out.

Its walls were covered with running blood,
But what could I do?
It was there, standing with its own pride.
Hideous pride that wasn't wanted,
Well, pride that I didn't want!

Leanne Hewitt (13)
Kilkeel High School

Jaguar

With a gentle touch you can hear the purr,
When driven to anger,
You can hear the roar!
As it speeds into the night,
Its bright eyes light up,
With perfect body shape
And smooth, slick lines.
Eye-catching shape,
It zooms by.
This big cat can twist and turn,
But then,
A sudden stop
Silence.

Neil Stevenson (13)
Kilkeel High School

Balloon

It floats around all over the place,
In a bubble of air - going nowhere.
A bag of nothing - doing nothing.
It bumps into everything,
Then just floats away.
A silence, soft shape
It bangs into things.
Doesn't even realise what it has done.
As lifeless as a sleeping baby,
Even when it's awake!
It gets pushed around everywhere,
But isn't even aware what is happening.
It really needs to stay awake,
Although then again, it already is!

Grace Scott (14)
Kilkeel High School

The Bus

Wide open ocean, to be explored,
A quest for sustenance,
Through enfolding arms
Of waves and movement.

Deeper and deeper, travelling onwards,
Expanding hidden doors.
Enticing its nourishment in
To lead them astray.

The day quickly expires,
With a stomach left unfilled.
Hoping for tomorrow,
A new day for new prey.

Aimee Forsythe (13)
Kilkeel High School

Old Car

Dodos are not extinct
One still survives,
I laid eyes upon it last week,
Its glowing eyes staring, following me
Its poky beak raised slightly
The sharp, squeaky noise that it made as it moved
Ancient bodywork.
Too heavy for its feeble frame.
Nothing could shield me from its pure ugliness.
I couldn't bare it, so I hurried away.
It tried to follow me but I got away.
The car belongs in a museum
Not on the open road, for everyone to see.

Jonathan Ewart (13)
Kilkeel High School

The Bullet

It shoots out
Darting the corners,
Heading towards me
Its black, beady eyes staring at me.

When suddenly
It speeds up
And gets closer and closer.
I can now see the black and yellow,
Signs of danger,
Signs of caution.

The sting fiercely pierces into me,
The pain is quick and sharp.
Just like its master
The striped vermin has gone -
For now.

Melissa Nicholson (13)
Kilkeel High School

My First Football Game

Nerves, tension
Waiting for my eyes to explode
Out of my sockets.
One intensive game,
Like a tiger chasing its prey,
As my eyes erupt,
Eyeing the ball,
Controlling every movement,
Full time.

Jason McCulla (15)
Kilkeel High School

Fishing

Fishing is fun
Fishing is cool,
Beach casting
Fly-fishing
In a river,
Swing
Cast
Swing
Cast.
With a pal in the pool
Spinning the day away
Refill the reel
A new spool
Fishing is like riding a bike
Once you learn
You never forget.

Nathan Stewart (13)
Kilkeel High School

Dance Competition

Nervous, excited
Made a mistake,
Wish the ground would swallow me up.
Don't want to put a foot out of place.
It's as if I'm in the Army.
Judges scribble down notes and then decide
Who first place goes to!
Bright lights like fireballs blind my sight.
The beat of the bagpipes drowns out our beat,
End with a bow -
Breathe.

Kelly Forsythe (15)
Kilkeel High School

Pizza

It looks like a bumpy pancake,
With different toppings.
It smells like tomato
With cheese on top.
It feels like a rough, stony beach,
It has a burst of exquisite tastes.
Soft in the middle, hard on the outside.

Dean McKee (11)
Kilkeel High School

The Tree

Flinging its fingers at me,
trying to hold on,
plucking my jumper and trousers.
I pulled away, its nails
nipping deep into my skin.
I got out my knife and
slashed off one of its bony,
long fingers and made my way
up the rest of the tree.

Andrew Patterson (13)
Kilkeel High School

Spaghetti Bolognese

Looks like computer cables
Smells like tomatoes
Tastes hot and chewy
It makes my eyes water
Feels hard, when not cooked
Feels soft and mushy when it is.
Looks, feels, tastes, smells good.

Alanna Fitzpatrick (12)
Kilkeel High School

Pasta

It looks like a bowl
Packed with lumpy mountains,
It looks like a hot, sizzling sun.

It feels like it's crawling
Down your throat,
It feels like walking on jelly.

When you see it, it looks steamy,
When the tomato and basil
Smell gets to your nose,
It's good!

When the flavour hits your mouth
It tastes so good.
When it goes down, your tummy goes, 'Yum!'

Andrew Charleton (11)
Kilkeel High School

Potatoes!

They look like huge scoops of ice cream,
They even look like snowballs,
But when I put them in my mouth
They don't taste hard at all.

They are dirty and covered in mud,
But then get peeled or scrubbed and *scrubbed!*
You can have them boiled, mashed or fried,
But please *don't* knock them
Until you've tried them.

Lesley Ann Glenny (12)
Kilkeel High School

Military Machine

The military machine is still alive,
Searching place to place,
Standing high and well-equipped,
Ready to fire at any hit.
Shooting and firing,
What will happen?
Will the mission succeed?
Wearing his armour,
Coated in paint.
Can he possibly survive?
Oh no, look at this!
He's about to open fire,
Off he goes, doing his thing.
He's about to say goodbye.

Ryan Simpson (13)
Kilkeel High School

Delivering Leaflets!

On my face are tiny droplets,
As I walk down the street.
Ten pounds at a time.
In and out of driveways,
Hours seem to go on forever.
Screaming in my ear,
'Get this thing done!'
I pass houses,
Darkness falling upon us,
Cold all around.
Wind howling through my ears,
Miles set ahead of us,
I'll have to come back tomorrow.

Steven Cousins (14)
Kilkeel High School

What Will I Be When I Grow Up?

Two years ago,
I was in my bedroom
With my friend,
Who turned to me and said,
'What do you want to be?'
'A doctor!'
But now I'm thinking -
Too horrible,
Too much blood!
A hairdresser?
But then I thought -
Standing all the time,
So many people,
Cutting hair all the time,
Oh, and don't forget the fingers too!
Don't get much money . . .
Getting older . . .
Changed my mind.

Vicky Wilson (13)
Kilkeel High School

Hunger!

When I hear my stomach rumble
I know what it could say
It would say, 'Give me lovely food,
Give me lovely food, every day.'
It feels smooth, it feels rough
It looks all torn, all dirty and tough
But when it comes to eating,
I never hear anyone complain
They just eat it with a smile on their face
And you never see it again!

Adrian Annett (14)
Kilkeel High School

The Friend I Never Had

Kind,
Sweet,
Nice to meet,
Always smiling,
Walked past her,
Had to smile!
But she turned evil,
Cruel and unkind.
Talked about me
Behind my back.
She always seemed so nice,
But now she has gone bad like a rotten egg.
Can't smile back now.
What she said about me
Was evil,
Mean.
I hate her so much.
Like turned to hate!
Friend turned to enemy!

Lisa Graham (14)
Kilkeel High School

Footballs

It's small and round,
It makes a thud when kicked,
It has a vile taste.
It's hard and light,
It lives in a store room.
It smells like grass,
If it could speak, it would say, 'Ouch!'
The pain of being . . . a football.

Nikki Scott (14)
Kilkeel High School

Young Writers - Great Minds From Co Down

My Animal

My animal has a big, black nose
Big, blue eyes
And big, long toes

He swings from tree to tree
And when he wants a rest
He sits upon my knee

He smells just a little bit
It doesn't bother me
But some people have a fit

He's a very lazy thing
He sleeps nearly all day long
He lives in a hot
Place called Australia

He's a soft teddy bear
He's a koala bear.

Gary Johnston (12)
Kilkeel High School

Love

It's in the deepest love of the heart
at the love shack
It sounds like an engine purring;
purr, purr, purr!
It tastes like fresh strawberries,
It feels like nothing I've ever felt before.
It looks like a super model
It smells like a rose.
It would say, 'Go over and talk to her.'

Matthew Hazard (12)
Kilkeel High School

My Dog Tipsy

Her short, black, shining hair
Glistening in the sun,
Chocolate brown eyes,
Always full of fun.

A snow white tipped tail,
Making it a feature,
That's how she got her name,
She's a beautiful creature.

You see her name is Tipsy,
A really cute pup,
I hope she's still as much fun
When she grows up.

Alastair Parke (12)
Kilkeel High School

Boredom

Boredom, boredom, boredom,
Looks like a dull grey day
In the middle of winter,
Sounds like the wind whistling
Through the trees,
And tastes like sour milk from
The year before.
It feels like French on a Tuesday morning,
It lives within the school,
If it could speak, it would say,
'School is so boring.'

David Hill (14)
Kilkeel High School

Football

The hustle and bustle of the players,
Readying themselves for battle,
While the fans outside
Burst with anticipation,
Singing their songs,
Like a bunch of drunks.
The pushing and shoving
To see their favourite eleven players
Burst onto the pitch.

Simon McKee (15)
Kilkeel High School

Chicken

From an egg to a hen, you grow for me,
From living to dead, you die for me,
From fluffy to bald, you're plucked for me,
From a packet to an oven, you're cooked for me,
From a plate to my stomach you're energy for me,
From me to you, thank you.

Christopher Annett (13)
Kilkeel High School

Love

Looks like red heart-shaped balloons floating high,
Music of lovers, slow moving songs.
Taste of sticky caramel, heart-shaped chocolates, melting
A warming sensation.
It lives deep in the centre of your heart.
A scent of gorgeous perfume and rich aroma of scented candles
And it would say three little words . . . 'I love you.'

Karen Speers (15)
Kilkeel High School

Old Trafford

We arrived at the magical stadium,
Mouths dropped open with astonishment everywhere.
What world were we in,
A real or a magical world?
I'm still not sure.
We took our seats, the players walked onto the pitch,
Deafening cheers broke out as the players took their mark.
A dreadful start, but not for long.
The drama began!
Everyone took to their feet,
The ball crashed into the back of the net!
Roars of excitement filled the stadium,
Van Nistelrooy scored again.
What a game it turned out to be.
The match came to a thunderous end.
Who won? You tell me.

Mark Graham (15)
Kilkeel High School

Anger

It looks like a raging bull,
It smells like the singeing
aftersmell of fireworks.
It's an indescribable feeling.
If anger had a colour, it would
Be dark red with flashes of orange.
It lives inside everyone, getting stronger,
Waiting to be released.
It tastes like the hottest of any chilli.
If it could talk, it would say,
'Why, you little . . . !'

William Hanna (14)
Kilkeel High School

Friend

She's nice,
She's a friend,
A best friend!
Suddenly . . .
Hates me,
Talks about me!
Hitting,
Hurting,
Dog barking,
Dishes clanging,
TV blaring,
Can't think!
All alone,
Friend turned enemy,
Why me?
New place,
New friend,
Happiness!

Rebekah Heelham (13)
Kilkeel High School

Pretty Flowers

Lots of pretty flowers; small
or tall. All flowers are neat
and sweet. They come in
funny shapes.

The colours are beautiful,
fiery hot reds, pretty, bright
pinks and ice-cold blues.
They smell good like a
summer's day, they look
good and they make you happy.

Melanie Newell (14)
Kilkeel High School

Nature

Nature has a way
A way that should stay
A way that should be around forever
Because nature is clever

Nature is the cool wind
That hits your new Mercedes Benz
It's the raindrop that hits your cheek
During those hours you cannot speak

Nature is the rainbow
Shining through the window
It's the light that shines so bright
Day after day.

Gregory McCullough (13)
Kilkeel High School

Scared

Looks like a black cloud with
two big, evil eyes.
It sounds like a deep, heavy
voice going into your ears.
It tastes like burnt toast
that's cold in your mouth.
It feels like one hundred
pins sticking into you.
It lives in your attic waiting
for you to be alone.
It smells like overcooked
cabbage in a dirty pot.
It would say, 'I'm going to get you!'

Ruth Sloan (12)
Kilkeel High School

Pork Chops

They come in different sizes,
They come in different shapes,
They come in different flavours,
They really do taste great.
They are so very juicy,
And also chewy too.
We fry them or we grill them,
And serve them on a plate.

Andrew Gordon (12)
Kilkeel High School

Demon

D readed creature
E vil
M onstrous
O utrageous
aN noying

Andrew Park (12)
Kilkeel High School

Night

I see darkness
All over the night,
Except for the moon,
Which is like a floating ball in the sky,
And the stars are bits of glitter,
With happiness
Sparkling down on me,
The owls hoot,
Shivering with cold,
As the howling wind, like a giant,
Takes a long, sleepy yawn.

Phillip Hanna (13)
Kilkeel High School

Finally Free

Who knows? Who cares?
I didn't want Him.
Why would He want me?
Big and great,
Distant,
Hardly for me!

Heard the story;
A garden,
A cross,
Agony,
Why?
For me!

My eyes were open.
My heart was free.
It was all out of love for me.
Friend!
Saviour!
Lord!

Avril Edgar (17)
Kilkeel High School

My School Trip

When I was in P7,
I was the age of eleven.

Last year I went to Explorers
I sat with William Morris.

We learned about sharks,
I got full marks.

We went down under the sea,
There were big sharks, they scared me.

Gary Brown (11)
Kilkeel High School

The Tayto Factory

We looked at his chair,
But MrTayto wasn't there

We cried out, 'Where are you?'
But he wasn't about,

They told us not to worry,
But we were in a hurry.

Suddenly he burst through the door,
And let out a big roar.

He said, 'Go with the team, they'll show you around.'
We walked down a corridor and a flavouring room we found.

Prawn cocktail, salt and vinegar, cheese and onion and bacon.
All different flavours were there for the taking.

People in white coats, hair in white nets,
Clean hands, no place for smoking and no place for pets.

We watched potatoes being sliced,
Fried up and diced

Sorted, bagged and labelled.
Ready for your table

The tour was now over, the end of the day.
'Thanks!' to Mr Tayto and staff, we all say!

Adam Blakley (11)
Kilkeel High School

Ogre

O verly sized,
G rotesque,
R aging,
E nergetic.

Matthew Graham (13)
Kilkeel High School

Killowen

It was such fun in Killowen
Especially canoeing, when I was rowing.
Bouldering was fun,
And was loved by everyone!
Even though it was last,
It was still a blast.
First we did the rope traverse
I'm glad it wasn't done in reverse.
Abseiling wasn't frightening
I went down like lightning!
The food was yummy,
In my tummy.
I didn't want to go,
I cried, 'No, no, no!'

Rachel Haugh (11)
Kilkeel High School

Happiness

Some people take happiness for granted
Or try to use other things to get happiness,
But happiness is the simple things in life.
Happiness is having something to eat,
Happiness is having somewhere to sleep at night.
Happiness is playing with your dog,
Happiness is hearing the birds sing.
Happiness is watching the sunset fall.
Happiness is walking on the beach.
Happiness is forgiving someone,
Happiness is being grateful for life.

Laura-Jane Reilly (11)
Kilkeel High School

Time Machine

If I could turn back time
I would make you truly mine,
No stupid flings
Or throwing things,
Our relationship would be fine.

No storming rows
Or raising brows,
No freaking out,
Or creeping about,
Our relationship would be fine.

If only time could change the past
And we would let the good times last,
Then you might see
The real me,
And our relationship would be fine.

Kathryn Edgar (14)
Kilkeel High School

The Chinese

There it was,
Sitting on the table.
It smelt so good,
'Come on in, I won't hurt!'
I could not resist it, I took a bite . . .
The rice was dancing on my tongue,
A couple of minutes later
I had it all eaten.
I took a big, big drink of Coke
To wash it down.

Colin Spence
Kilkeel High School

Change Of Heart

Always tired,
Early mornings,
Crowded bus.

Bell ringing,
Talking, shouting, banging.

Clock ticking,
Kids screaming,
Teachers shouting,
Doors banging,
Kids running.

A lot of noise,
No one listens . . .

Break,
Lunch,
Quick,
Hurry.

Bell ringing,
Teachers shouting,
Kids screaming,
Back to class.

Ten past three,
There's the bus, run.

School, it never changes.
We always want to be back when at home.
When at home we want to be at school.

Nicola Poole (17)
Kilkeel High School

Sweets

Sweets are sugary, fizzy, tasty,
But for your teeth, they are nasty!
Everybody loves them. Everyone wants them.
There's not a child in the world who hates them.

There are so many different types;
Jellies, gummies, brown chocolate or white.
Your only dream's melting in your mouth,
A rainbow of colours all at once!

It's everyone's excuse to cheer themselves up,
Eating chocolates at the telly, with some hot cocoa in your cup.
But, what would kids do if it was during the war
And sweets were on rations, just like before?

Lynda Annett (13)
Kilkeel High School

Roller Coaster

Bright summer's day!
People were sick,
They'd just been on the roller coaster.
I was about to go on.
Awaiting my doom!
We started moving;
My legs like jelly.
No going back.
Like a flash of lightning
It was over.
It was brilliant.
I'm going again.

Gregory Glenny (13)
Kilkeel High School

Pizza

It tastes cheesy, with a hint of vegetables through it,
Finishing off with a crispy crust around the edge.
It looks messy, with bright colours
Sprinkled over the top,
With a hard crust around the edge,
Which is like a huge wall surrounding it.
It smells like a great big bowl of
Vegetables being cooked up.
Its texture is soft and spongy in the middle.
It makes me feel like I have been
On a fast roller coaster,
As it is so refreshing.

Rachel Wackett (11)
Kilkeel High School

Love

Love is like a lump of gold,
Hard to get and hard to hold.
Of all the girls I've met,
You're the one I won't forget.

Because you are funny,
Worthy, loyal and true,
And you are always there
For me to talk to.
You cheer me up when I am down,
You make me smile when I have a frown.

Out of all the rest, you are the best.

William Gracey (14)
Kilkeel High School

In Sweet Decline

I thought you'd always be there,
No matter what you'd say,
But now wraiths emasculate
And emaciate the sea.

Feathers gather in my hands,
Like cherry blossom dreams.
I want to read you like a book
And tear you at the seams.

Your skin is alabaster,
Your lips speak of sanguine floods,
But now my tears flow in crimson,
Weeping bitter blood.

Stars shine lifeless
Up above,
Necromantic testaments
To our failed and rotting love.

Daniel Smith (17)
Kilkeel High School

Painting The Boats

During the summer,
Working with my dad,
Painting the boats,
Painting for days.
I felt a shot of pain!
I went home
I laid down,
Got to thinking,
Stay at this job.
No!
I can't stick it,
Too boring!

Adrian Graham (13)
Kilkeel High School

Stirling

Stirling was really fun,
All the fights, all the music,
All the shops, all the shoes,
All the tops, all the trousers,
All the socks, all the skirts,
All the presents, all the friends,
All the places, all the fun.

Stirling would have been more fun
If there were more people,
If there were all my new friends,
If there were TVs,
If there was more time to shop,
If everyone joined in all the things,
If the high school boys were there.

Stirling was more fun because there was
A lot of shops,
A lot of people,
A lot of things to do,
A lot of shoes,
A lot of fun things to do.

Rebekah Blue (12)
Kilkeel High School

A Lonely Boat Ride

In a rough lane of water,
A large fishing boat sails through the waves.
Strong men cast out the nets,
They draw the nets in and count the catch,
A net full of shining mackerel.
They could see the great beam from the lighthouse,
The light glimmered on the top of the water.
They could see the moonlight,
So they set off for the harbour, by the
Reflection of the moon on the water.

Andrew Cummins (14)
Kilkeel High School

Pretence

How could she?
Does she not realise?
We know!
Grinning,
Arms outstretched,
What can we do but respond?
But we all know.
Just making a fool of herself.
What lies - it's all been lies!
Everything she said,
What can we believe now?
So fake. Everything fake!
But it's not her fault . . .
Or is it?
False smiles. False laughs.
We can see it all now of course.
Back then it was different
Best we know. Sad though,
Things can never be the same.
Just keep thinking, it will soon be over,
And we won't have to pretend.
Soon,
But not yet.

Jayne Scott (18)
Kilkeel High School

Happiness

Happiness is love, joy, peace and comfort.
Happiness is like the sun shining through.
Everyone feels happiness inside,
Like love shining as bright as a star.
Happiness is people who are kind and loving.
Happiness warms the heart!

Heather Speers (11)
Kilkeel High School

Cream Buns With Chocolate Trimmings!

As a boy named Charlie was walking down the street,
He found a shiny shilling laying at his feet.
He put it in his pocket and took it to the shop,
Hoping he wouldn't be seen by the local cop.
As Charlie ran to get his favourite bar,
Sadly he was knocked down by a car.

As he lay on the hospital bed,
Thoughts of chocolate grew in his head.
A cream bun with chocolate trim,
All this temptation began to seduce him.
As he dreamt of the creamy taste in his mouth,
He heard a rumble from somewhere south.

He couldn't take it any longer,
He was being overruled by his hunger.
He broke from his bed,
With sweet thoughts of chocolate in his head.
He ran towards the shop
And didn't dare stop!

As he busted through the door,
He thought of his belly all empty and sore.
Looking at the different treats was fun,
But all he wanted was his cream bun.
He bought a cream bun with chocolate trimming,
And that was the end of Charlie's silver shilling.

Rachel Johnston (12)
Kilkeel High School

Eagle

Eyes as red as blood,
My claws as sharp as razor blades.
I swoop like a falling brick.
I wait for the slightest movement
To make my kill.
I own the sky!

William Poole (12)
Kilkeel High School

Young Writers - Great Minds From Co Down

Pizza!

All different types of pizza
In the shop you buy,
And every time it's not on the menu,
I let out a huge, big sigh.
They're by far my favourite food,
Pepperoni and cheese with a crispy crust,
Oh just thinking about it
Makes my tummy want to bust.
Hot and spicy, my mouth is on fire,
Run upstairs to get some water,
Gulp it down with all my might!
When it's finished and it's all done,
I can't wait till next Monday
To get another one.

Jade Lurring (12)
Kilkeel High School

Pizza

Crispy, tasty, spicy food,
I love it, it is so good.
It is as round as the sun
And as hot as fire.
It smells so delicious
It makes my mouth water.
It is so bumpy and soft,
But it is still crispy.
It makes me feel so hungry,
Like I want to eat it.

Orla Corbett (11)
Kilkeel High School

My Job

Teaching,
An enjoyable and exciting job,
An interesting and fulfilling career.
I have always wanted to be a teacher.
It's been a dream of mine
Since I was nine!

However, my work experience in a school
Changed my thoughts completely,
It seemed like too much hard work,
And too much time in a classroom.
Too much chatter and noise,
Too many girls and boys!

Impossible, it is now,
For me to be a teacher.
But I will have to wait and see
What job the future holds for me!

Lindsey McConnell (17)
Kilkeel High School

Suicide

A big, dark, black cloud
Screaming constantly inside.
Burning hot fuel
Trying to escape
From the darkest cave with no end,
The most evil feeling
Screaming, 'Kill me, kill me!'

Gary Morris (13)
Kilkeel High School

Potatoes And Meat

For dinner, meat is mouth-watering,
And potatoes are delicious.
Cooked meat looks tempting,
And potatoes roasted golden brown.
Walk into the kitchen
And you weaken at the knees,
With the roast in the oven
And the spuds in the pan.
The texture of the spuds
Is like clouds in the sky.
Red meat, fine and silky,
Potatoes like cotton wool,
And meat tender as a sponge.

Stephen Gordon (12)
Kilkeel High School

Pizza

It tastes mouth-watering,
And it tastes really, really cheesy.
It looks very, very juicy, mouth-watering
And very, very tasty.
It smells like melted cheese
On its own.
It makes me feel
All warm inside.
It feels rough on the bottom
And slippery on top.

William Smyth (11)
Kilkeel High School

Shopping

People were rushing about
Like wild animals.
They must have thought
The shops were not going to open the next day.
Shopping was never like that before.
They were shouting, screaming almost,
Yelling from the rooftops,
But now
I'm one of those people who love to shop,
Dashing around
To find the next good bargain.
Shopping is amazing,
Shopping will never be the same again.

Louise Houston (14)
Kilkeel High School

Pizza

Pizza is a big, round planet,
floating in the air.
It's hot, crispy, spicy, and smells like
All my favourite flavours mixed together.
It tastes like a cloud full of sweets.
On the top, it is like a soft marshmallow,
and underneath it is like a hard, crispy crisp;
a round wafer,
a sun twisting round and round.

Sarah McConnell (11)
Kilkeel High School

Dolphin

I am a
wave maker,
smooth jumper,
lullaby singing;
I mean no harm.

I know
the nets of the tuna ships,
to toss and turn in the sea,
so calm and gentle,
when all sea animals meet
at dusk and dawn,
the name of the dolphin.
I mean no harm.

Megan Wortley (12)
Kilkeel High School

Pizza

It looks like a colourful flower,
It tastes like hot, crusty vegetables,
It smells like hot, creamy tomatoes,
Its cheese reminds me of the gleaming sun.
There are so many toppings; cheese, tomato and ham.
It's a perfect snack, it's a perfect deal.
You can practically eat it for any meal.
You eat right through till you come to the crust,
You'll eat so much you will eventually bust!

Anna Barbour (12)
Kilkeel High School

Snake

Like a hidden warrior
Waiting to kill,
Razor-sharp senses
To help make its move.

Its stomach, a prison,
Once you're in, you can't get out.
Poison is its weapon,
To help strike down its prey.

Its markings are like a warning sign,
Once you see them, you'd better run.
It will always be there,
Sitting, listening and waiting.

Gareth Robinson (12)
Kilkeel High School

All Mixed Up

A sheet of coloured paper,
A puzzle all mixed up in your head,
An unorganised English homework,
Words scattered all over the page.
A newly-found dictionary with new words,
Never to be discovered.
A book starting at the back and ending at the front,
A hard feeling, of not knowing whether to
Cry, laugh, scream, shout, smile or walk out.
These are mixed emotions.

Jessica Nugent (11)
Kilkeel High School

Vegetable Rap Poem

Vegetables are so good for you,
You do not realise what they do.
Some look like trees, but taste real nice,
I must admit I like mine diced.

They come in lots of different colours,
I wish I could keep track of the others.
You eat them raw, you eat them cooked,
You can choose lots of recipes from a book.

Even though onions make you cry,
They keep your heart healthy so you won't die.
Carrots, peppers and chillies too,
They all will do the best for you.

Hannah Thompson (12)
Kilkeel High School

Untitled

At first, annoying,
Every stupid little action,
Giggling as I walked into a room,
Stopped talking, or even left the room,
Paranoid and obsessed,
I learnt to ignore,
But after a move, we get on OK.
A bit annoying,
But forced together,
We get on quite well.

Stacey Holmes (15)
Kilkeel High School

Chocolate

Chocolate,
I wish I had some of that,
The delicious stuff
That melts on your tongue.
As soon as you rip off
That golden wrapper,
You become addicted.
Brown and white, soft or hard,
An essential part of life!
I don't know what would happen to the world
If there was no *chocolate!*

Adele McConnell (12)
Kilkeel High School

Hallowe'en

H aunted house!
A lways scares you!
L ollipops!
L ights in pumpkins!
O gres!
W erewolves!
E erie noises!
E veryone is spooked!
N asty witches!

Simon Herron (12)
Kilkeel High School

Fire

Different colours,
Red, blue, orange and green,
Roaring like an angry bear,
Raging through a farmer's ditch,
As smoke clouds fill the sky,
People come and stare.

Fire engines racing down,
Tearing past the noisy crowd,
Shooting water into the air,
Trying to tame the frightening glare.

Thomas Nixon (14)
Kilkeel High School

My Friend

A broken heart,
A lonely child,
Tears of sadness
In my time of sorrow.
Dark and lonely days ahead
Without your loving hand.
Oh why, oh why did you leave me?
You were my friend, my sister,
My second mum,
I love you and I miss you.
Why did you have to go away?
My friend, my sister,
My second mum,
Don't leave me alone.
I'll miss you.
Tears of sorrow and tears of sadness,
You were the best nanny I ever had.
As time goes by and darkness lifts,
The sunshine of memories
Our everlasting gift.

Mauricia Croan (11)
St Columbanus College, Bangor

Tikka And I

I ran and ran until I fell,
Tikka with me.
I cried and cried until I whined,
Tikka with me.

My dad said she had to go,
We both cried at him.
She didn't mean to hurt the dog,
All she wanted to do was to play.

I shouted and shouted;
I ran and ran;
While crying all the time.

She had to go,
We all knew it,
But all she wanted was to stay and play.

I wanted to introduce you,
Tikka, meet them.
This is Tikka,
My pet tiger.

Emma McColl (15)
St Columbanus College, Bangor

My First Day At School

First day in school,
I was so excited,
I thought I was really cool.
My teacher had a nice smile,
She was so kind and caring,
She taught us about sharing.
It was like a paradise,
All we did was play,
The whole way through the day.
I loved to play in the sand,
My friends would always try and bury my hands!

Joanne Hamilton (15)
St Columbanus College, Bangor

What A Horrible Day

Oh, what a horrible day,
As I went out to play,
It seemed OK throughout the day
But when night came,
It didn't feel the same.
I walked to the shop with my friend Claire.
I'll tell you the scare we had there.
As we walked in to pick our sweets,
We turned to face two masked men
With guns in their hands.
My heart sank, I started to cry,
I worried if I would maybe die!
They held the gun to our heads and said,
'Don't move or you will soon be dead.'
They emptied the till into a sack,
I collapsed to the ground and put my hands to my face.
My heart began to race, they ran off,
The shop fell silent . . .
I looked at Claire, she looked at me,
We fell into each other's arms and cried.
We were so glad it was over,
And that nobody *died!*

Leah Devanney (12)
St Columbanus College, Bangor

Taking Steps

They were the happiest days of my life,
Unforgettable memories painted in my head.
How can I not forget playing in my toy car
And the pain of getting hurt?
Scoring my first ever goal was the best
As I celebrated putting my vest over my head.
Over the years I have grown,
But deep down inside my past has stayed.

Steven Rogan (15)
St Columbanus College, Bangor

Childhood

I was the child that played all the pranks,
I was the child that was always a clown,
I was the child that wanted toy tanks,
I was the child that got lost in town.

I was the boy who never got in trouble,
I was the boy who thought he was a spy,
I was the boy who tried making his money double,
I was the boy who thought he could fly.

I was the teen who loved the army,
I was the teen who loved school,
I was the teen who's a bit boring,
I was the teen whose attitude was cool.

I am the man who loves his job,
I am the man who loves his family,
I am the man who's not a slob,
I am the man who sleeps calmly.

Matthew Morris (15)
St Columbanus College, Bangor

Owl

A shadow is floating through the moonlight,
Its wings don't make a sound.
Its claws are long, its beak is bright,
Its eyes try all the corners of the night.

It calls and calls; all the air swells and heaves
And washes up and down like water.
The ear that listens to the owl believes
In death. The bat lives beneath the eaves.

The mouse beside the stone is still as death,
The owl's air washes over them like water.
The owl goes back and forth inside the night
And the night holds its breath.

Natalie McCloud (12)
St Columbanus College, Bangor

Young Writers - Great Minds From Co Down

Crying At The Littlest Things

Bashing of knees
And scraping of elbows,
Crying at the littlest things.

Not getting your way,
Not allowed to stay up,
Crying at the littlest things.

Not getting toys
For Christmas or birthdays,
Crying at the littlest things.

Not understanding
How magic tricks work,
Crying at the littlest things.

Screaming at movies
That are on TV,
Crying at the littlest things.

Dominic McAvera (15)
St Columbanus College, Bangor

Dad's Army

Journey up the tree-lined path
On my way to school,
My dad was so far away,
Out of our big cage.
I've always wondered what it would be like
To step a foot out of that gate.
I was always used to everything in hand,
The park out the door and friends up the road.
It's my dad's military parade tomorrow,
Oh how scared he must be!
But in my eyes my dad is my idol and hero,
And I'm as proud as can be!

Lynsey Reilly (16)
St Columbanus College, Bangor

Mother - Father

My father - mother are nice,
Every day they give me advice,
When they give me something,
I say, 'Thank you very much.'
In return they say, 'We love you very much.'
They help me in my homework,
I help them in their housework.
Sometimes they scold me,
Sometimes they encourage me.
We have to be good in studies,
And behave well so that
No one says we are naughty.
We don't go astray,
So that their hearts may break.
To be good children should be our aim,
So that they never have to look down in shame.
We should make them feel proud of us,
Happy we will make them thus.

Merin D'cruz (12)
St Columbanus College, Bangor

Untitled

Happy memories with my big dad,
Having loads of fun.
While I was glad
He took me out to the zoo
And took me to get ice cream too,
Now we are apart,
I want it more,
I really enjoy it and so did he.
I wish we could do it
Like we used to do,
But all I've got are my capture photos.

Leanne Smith (16)
St Columbanus College, Bangor

What's Happening To Me?

One day I was in the car,
I started to scream,
A car heading towards us,
It didn't stop and see,
It hit us with a thump.
The car started spinning around
And around.
Thoughts were going through my head,
What's going to happen to me?
See the policeman come running to the scene,
See the ambulance lights
In front of me.
So blue, so bright.
What's happening to me?
The fright of it all made me cry.
Carried on a stretcher to the ambulance
By an ambulance guy,
People gathered around, sitting, staring,
Looking at me.
What's happening to me?
I wonder why
It had to be me?
I woke up, it was a dream,
I'm glad that didn't happen to me!

Clare Houston (13)
St Columbanus College, Bangor

Children

Laughing at the silliest things,
Acting like a plane, pretending I have wings,
Always causing aggravation,
Simplest things cause such fascination.
Always fighting,
Scratching, crawling, punching, biting,
Letting on it wasn't me.
Climbing up the tallest tree,
Always crying,
When in trouble, always lying,
Running, playing, jumping, leaping,
Only peaceful when we're sleeping.

Michael Brown (16)
St Columbanus College, Bangor

A Heap Of Hates

I don't like people picking their noses,
Or going shopping for fancy clothes.
I hate the taste of sauce, and beef burgers.
Boring history digs and cigarette leftovers.
Don't like beans,
Tennis on TV and homework too.
Pens bursting in your hands,
Or Man U.
Out in the garden playing football,
Missing a good shot and breaking a flower pot.
These are the things I hate,
Better go, 'cause I'm gonna be late.

Conor Boden (11)
St Malachy's High School, Castlewellan

What Every Girl Wants

Fanta Lemon straight from the fridge.
Letting my dog in the house.
Dancing, singing, playing tin whistles all night.
Lying watching EastEnders and munching on crisps.
Going on holidays, seeing the sights.
Going to the pizza place, so cool.
Reading Mizz, Dare and Sugar.
Canoeing and rock climbing are my fave sports.
Water fights with the neighbours.
Doing art and getting messy.
These are what every girl wants.

Anna Brogan (11)
St Malachy's High School, Castlewellan

My Favourite Things

Love Saturday mornings,
The feeling is just great,
Wake up and think,
No school today!
Like Father Ted and Dougal,
They would make anyone laugh.
I enjoy F1, it is a dangerous motor sport
But I enjoy it.
Going up the mountain.
We walk four to five miles,
But that is up hill.
Going to football training in Hilltown pitch.
It is good craic.

John Gallagher (11)
St Malachy's High School, Castlewellan

These Are A Few Of My Favourite Things

Love getting home from school on a Friday,
The house is always nice and tidy.
Waking up on a Saturday morning,
Remembering that there is no school for another two days.
Love Diet Coke straight from the fridge.
Going on holidays is the best thing I ever did.
Going to the swimming pool is fabulous too.
Love going to a brand new school.
The smell of Mum's lovely stuffing,
Excitement grows as Christmas is coming.
Watching Coronation Street and eating my dinner.
Listening to a good pop band is a winner.
Playing on the beach with the sand.
Feeling the rays of sun as my skin is tanned.
These are a few of my favourite things.

Rachel Dickson (11)
St Malachy's High School, Castlewellan

I Don't Want That

I don't like seeing sick animals or people,
And 7UP tastes horrible too.
I hate people munching on chips,
When I am in the line and feeling hungry.
I think chicken is disgusting and I'm not fond of peas.
Toffee is horrible and cream is too.
I don't like getting up at 7.15am on weekdays,
Or having lots of homework to do.
I don't like dark colours like brown or black.
These are a few things I hate,
What about you?

Rosemary O'Loughlin (12)
St Malachy's High School, Castlewellan

Pet Hates

Hate the smell of rotten eggs,
Hate the smell of burnt-out fags.
Hate standing in the tuck shop queuing for hours,
Hate the smell of dead flowers.
Hate Christmas exams and summer tests,
Going shopping for my wee sister's vests.
Hate a cold shower in the morning,
And sitting in form class, it's so boring!
Hate the smell of vanilla candles,
Hate the sting of jaggy nettles.
Hate the colour of boring grey,
I'd rather have a walk along Dundrum Bay.

Rebecca McGreevy (12)
St Malachy's High School, Castlewellan

Grumpy Young Man

I hate it when I get sunburnt,
    Even when I get really hurt.
I hate it when the doors need oiling,
    The smell of sprouts boiling.
I hate soppy movies,
    Especially lumpy smoothies.
I hate cold nights
    And flying big kites.
I hate the game of tig
    And the smell of a pig.
I hate straight cars
    And rock hard chocolate bars.

Gerard Corrigan (12)
St Malachy's High School, Castlewellan

Freedom

Love the feeling on a Friday at twenty to four,
Smelling Mum's chips as I'm coming through the door.
Watching good films on the telly,
Eating lots of ice cream and jelly.
Coming outside and seeing a hot summer sun,
Playing with my friends, having lots of fun.
Going to the local swimming pool,
Watching my brother act like a fool.
Playing with my friend's fluffy bunny,
My mum giving me lots of pocket money.
That's the end, but I could still say lots more,
Just don't have time, 'cause it's twenty to four.

Caoimhe Toner (12)
St Malachy's High School, Castlewellan

What I Like

Fanta Orange straight from the fridge,
Crispy brown chips for dinner,
Ice cream for dessert.
Watching Corrie on a weekday night,
Going to the cinema to see the latest films.
At the end of the school day, feeling free,
Reading my books before I go to sleep.
Watching 'Friends' any day of the week.
Having snowball fights with my mates.
Getting a gravy chip from Zebedee's.
Going to Newry shopping on a Saturday morning.

Roisin Malone (12)
St Malachy's High School, Castlewellan

It's A Girl Thing!

Apples, bananas, cherries and pears,
Love a night out with the girls.
Dancing, walking, playing ball,
Also singing in the school hall.
Waking up on a Saturday morning,
Also doing lots of drawing.
Love my daddy's shepherd's pie,
Hate when Mum calls my sister a cutie pie.
Love when the bell rings at twenty to four,
Love to go home and lie on the floor.
Like to watch TV all day long,
Then I go and sing some songs.
Like lots of furry things,
Also like my clothes to bling.
Now you know just what I like,
I also like to play on my bike.

Carol-Anne Magennis (11)
St Malachy's High School, Castlewellan

Junk Food

What is junk food?
Everything you like . . .
Pizza, chips and Mars Delights.

All the things we like to eat
Are full of calories and too sweet.

Every day we hear the sound,
'Healthy eating', and we all frown.
We like things that taste so nice,
Things that wet our appetite.

Greens and fruits are boring food,
We might as well be eating wood.
Pizza, chips and Mars Delights,
Oh yes, oh yes, don't they taste right!

Andrew Dines (14)
Strangford College

A Favourite Food?

I don't have a favourite food,
There's lots I like the same,
But when it comes to dinnertime,
The choice is pretty lame.

The spiciest is curry,
The fattiest is chips,
The most disgusting one of all,
Is probably a pizza mix.

Spaghetti is Italian,
Escargot is French,
When I go home, I don't know
What's waiting on the bench.

Maybe it's something different,
Something I've never had.
I'm too late, there's nothing left,
Who's eaten, but my dad!

Sarah Gregory (13)
Strangford College

What Lies Beneath?

The small but deep, meaningful teardrops
Flows down your soft skin.
Shedding strong emotions,
Which words cannot explain.

The transparent teardrop is full of
Heartfelt secrets,
With thought and feeling
Which only a teardrop can say.

The droplet of water
That falls from the eye
Can say everything,
Without speaking a word.

Melissa Perkins (13)
Strangford College

Young Writers - Great Minds From Co Down

A Doll's Life

She sits and stares
without a word,
day after day,
time after time.

I wonder what she thinks about
and how she passes the day
without any talk or play.

Now gathering dust, she's forgotten and old,
her paradise now faded,
to start with a life of leisure and love,
and now to be filled with hatred.

The girl she once knew and loved
abandoned her and left,
and now to sit upon that shelf
she probably welcomes death.

For not to be with a friend while dying,
day after day,
time after time.

Amanda Davies (14)
Strangford College

Mashed Potato

Mashed potato is my favourite food,
I really like it, it tastes really good.

I mix it all up with loads of brown sauce,
If I could never have mashed potato, it would be a great loss.

Mashed potato is my favourite food,
I really like it, it tastes really good.

Ryan Fox (13)
Strangford College

Why?

I was dumped in a horrible place no one should be,
Stuck somewhere instead of being free.
There's not even one familiar face,
I definitely knew this wasn't my place.

Hunger struck me day by day,
How could anyone be treated this way?
A small bowl of rice and a glass of dirty water was all I got,
They may as well have left me to rot.

At night I look up at the beautiful glowing moon,
Hoping a caring family would adopt me soon.
As I imagine having a proper family every night,
It brings a tear to my eye,
Besides, what else could I do, but cry?

Here I am, hungry, cold and alone,
I just want a family of my own!
I ask myself every second of every day,
Why was I dumped in this horrible place?
Why?

Sabrina McCullough (13)
Strangford College

My Favourite Food

My favourite food is chips,
Tomato ketchup as a dip.
Beans and chicken nuggets,
KFC in a bucket.

I never eat peas,
But give me a burger with peas.
I love a nice Chinese.
Can I have some more please?

Leigh Savage (13)
Strangford College

Strawberries And Kinder Bueno

I don't like many foods
But Kinder Buenos and strawberries are very good.
I wish my mum would buy them every day,
But she doesn't get enough pay.

My mum buys strawberries on a Sunday,
And Kinder Buenos on a Monday.
She says, 'Leave them for tea.'
But instead I grab them all for me!

I love strawberries when they're ripe,
Kinder Buenos I eat in one bite.
My brother says I'll get fat.
I shout at him, 'Shut up, you cheeky brat!'

Strawberries are best in summertime,
When served with cream and lots of wine!
Kinder Buenos are yummy at any time,
Especially when they're all mine!

Rebecca McKee (13)
Strangford College

Music

It's music to my ears,
Music that shouldn't be judged,
It's how we feel, the truth,
Accompanied by sharps and flats.

It's music to my ears,
Music that's so pure and sweet,
It's how it should be,
The sound of music that will last.

It's music to my ears,
Feelings that explode onto paper,
Sung by the sweetest voice,
Sung throughout the years.

Leeza Fitzsimmons (14)
Strangford College

No More Rain, No More Drizzle

The darkness fell so gently, but quickly,
For no one knew of terrors to arise.
People dashed to their homes in time of a whisper,
As rain battered on the windows in their eyes.

Many minutes turned into hours, and hours turned into days,
The water rose to mighty heights.
Like bugs, people scattered to the rooftops
For to see such horrible sights.

Suddenly through darkness peeped a hope of light,
For it was the sun at last.
The rain dribbled and spat until it died,
So quickly the skies lit up in a blast.

Many minutes then passed, and hours, and then days,
So the water dried into a sizzle.
People could run, walk, dance, without having to swim.
No more rain, no more drizzle.
No more rain, no more drizzle.

Philip Wright (13)
Strangford College

Grounded

Alone in my room is where I will sit,
Never before had I thrown such a fit.
They pushed and pushed, until I gave in,
By now I should know I never will win.
Everything's gone, no seeing good weather,
These next two weeks will feel like forever.
Just staring at walls, my butt falls asleep,
There is nothing but silence, not even a peep!
Every second goes by like a month or a year,
Why don't they realise I'm dying in here?
Knock, knock, you say that it's over,
Why I got up and was out like a bulldozer.

Maria Waugh (13)
Strangford College

The Power Cut

All of a sudden, out went the lights,
We were left in a room in the darkness of night.
No lights in the distance could we see,
What will we do, goodness me!

There was no watching TV or even listening to my favourite CD,
We tried to think of something to do, my family and me.
Out came the torches and candles for light,
Our dad went out into the cold, dark night.

We got out our games and began to play,
Then some minutes later the generator started - hooray!
Some lights and the TV were put on,
It was as if nothing was wrong.

I started to worry about having to go to bed,
When my cold, dark bedroom came into my head.
To my relief on came the power,
It seemed to be a very long three quarters of an hour.

Samantha Townley (13)
Strangford College

Food

I like sweets and chocolate and all sorts of food,
Ice cream and biscuits that make me feel good.
I like burgers and hot dogs and pizza, lots!
French fries and milk shakes, that come in small pots.

So I come home and raid the fridge, but guess what?
There's nothing in there but bread, that's the lot.
So I go upstairs to get my supplies,
To find my brother munching on pies.

He eats all the food and leaves me with none,
But one thing's for sure, he's definitely not won.
I'll make sure of that, oh yes I will,
Because when I go out, guess who'll get the bill?

Nikita Bewley (13)
Strangford College

Chan v Red Panda

Mr Chan and his wok
make a brilliant combination.
Creating lots of lovely food
to keep me from starvation!

Crispy spring rolls
wrapped up like presents . . . mmm.
Shredded chicken
bathed in sweet 'n' sour sauce . . . mmm.
Egg fried rice
and noodles . . . mmm.

But if
you are celebratin' . . .
the Red Panda's
the place to be eatin'!

Mikael Wilson (13)
Strangford College

If I Had A Wish

If I had a wish, I'd wish for a ring
That would make me a king.
I'd live in a huge castle,
Have lots of workers, so there's no trouble or hassle.

If I had a wish, I'd wish for a car
With two hundred horse-power.
Red fire up both sides,
Anyone would be able to come for a ride.

If I had a wish, I'd wish I could fly,
I'd fly high into the sky,
Then I'd fly to the moon,
But don't worry, I'd be back soon.

Michael Braniff (14)
Strangford College

Unforeseen Consequences

A red sea,
Fire all around,
Ash floating in the air,
The silence deafening.

Shaded faces glimpsed by the soulless cries of men
Wishing they could return back to the source
From which they came.
I look at these people
Thanking God it wasn't me.

Looking back, behind myself,
I see a red frozen water burial
And think, *was it a sign from Heaven or Hell?*
Or just Hell itself?

Andrew Danso (14)
Strangford College

The Outcast

I feel down, stressed,
Different from everyone.
Friendless, nobody wants me,
Those people don't even call me
By my first or surname.

They think my knees are dry,
Scabbed and cracked.
They think my uniform is out
When I walk about.

I feel so alone, cold and scared,
So hurt, so weepy.
Nobody wants me,
I am the *outcast.*

Stephanie Gouldie (13)
Strangford College

The Little Drops Of Heaven, Skittles!

Little drops of rain, falling down from Heaven,
Rainbow-coloured, staring brightly at you,
Lighting up like bulbs on a dance floor
Temptation sneaks up on you, ready to snatch
The packet like a hungry crocodile.
You have to give in,
There's no doubt about it.
The sweet, sugar flavour slides down your throat,
With you thinking crazily for more!
Ready to bounce into a deep, dark hole.
The crunching grinds against your teeth,
Sticking to them like a horse eating toffee.
You know it's coming to the end,
And fear the sound of an empty packet.
Devastated like a child, lost with no family,
But relief overcomes you
As a smile approaches your face,
Like the sunrise in the sky
Shining through the clouds.
You relax, as the room for one more is welcome,
Because there in front of you,
While your taste buds tingle,
Is that wondrous, sweet, fruit-flavoured
Drop of Heaven
In the corner, hiding.
Imagining those puppy-dog eyes staring at you,
Your heart pounds for the poor thing,
But . . . not for long,
As it joins the rest, soon enough,
In the deep, dark hole!

Alannah Turner (13)
Strangford College

Solo Dove

A solo dove
flies close by,
worried not,
for he is shy.
He tries to find,
but cannot seek,
for what he lacks
he cannot speak.
There are those who say
he has not lived,
he has no bird,
for love he'd give.
A light shines by,
he cannot see,
for what he likes
he'll never flee.
His love reflects
on what he sees,
he needs no girl
for him to be free.
For those who laugh,
they cannot see
that he is happy,
always free.

Jodie Dean (13)
Strangford College